LIVING LITURGY™

for Extraordinary Ministers of Holy Communion

Year B • 2018

Brian Schmisek
Diana Macalintal
Jay Cormier

LITURGICAL PRESS
Collegeville, Minnesota

www.litpress.org

ISSN 1933-3129

ISBN 978-0-8146-4650-2   ISBN 978-0-8146-4746-2 (ebook)

Presented to

_____

*in grateful appreciation
for ministering as an
Extraordinary Minister
of
Holy Communion*

_____

_____

(date)

USING THIS RESOURCE

Extraordinary typically refers to outstanding or exceptional.
But extraordinary ministers of Holy Communion are "extra"-
ordinary in the sense of "in addition to" the ordinary (as well as
being outstanding and exceptional!). Ordinary ministers of Holy
Communion are the ordained and those properly installed as
acolytes, usually seminarians. In parishes today there are simply
not enough "ordinary" ministers of Holy Communion, so we call
forth additional ministers, referred to as "extraordinary." Imagine how long the distribution of Communion would take if only
the ordained or seminarians were those who distributed! It is not
only because of need, however, that we have extraordinary ministers of Holy Communion. It is also by virtue of one's baptism.
We parishioners are grateful that so many baptized Christians
respond to the call to serve as extraordinary ministers of Holy
Communion. In so doing we are reminded that we are all holy, and
we are all called to ministry by virtue of our Christian baptism.

Preparing for This Ministry

Though different dioceses and parishes have slightly different
preparation requirements for those who would be extraordinary
ministers of Holy Communion, there is preparation nonetheless.
We hope that this book will be a source of reflection for such
preparation, and also for ongoing reflection throughout one's ministry. We know that it is not enough to simply attend a training
event and never look back. Each ministry of the church requires
regular prayer, reflection, reading, and thoughtfulness. This book
is intended to assist with that process by providing prayers and
reflection for each Sunday and for certain solemnities. This resource can also be used by groups who would like to share their
faith with questions that prompt discussion.

Holy Communion for the Homebound and Sick

In the New Testament Letter of James we learn about the concern
and care that the early Christians had for those members of their
community who were sick. Such care and concern was a hallmark
of Jesus' own ministry, and it has been a Christian charism ever
since. Each week there are parishioners who are not able to join

us for the liturgy, and so the Eucharist is brought to them as a sign of our unity. Extraordinary ministers of Holy Communion are often those who perform this ministry, and, in so doing, they extend the parish's reach to so many more fellow parishioners. This book is intended to be a resource for them as well.

Adapting This Resource for Holy Communion for the Homebound and Sick

The Communion rite (Ordinary Rite of Communion of the Sick) is provided as a separate publication to this book and enclosed within. Those who are extraordinary ministers of Holy Communion have undoubtedly been made familiar with this rite as part of their preparation. This book may be adapted for use with the rite, by sharing the gospel reflection, the prayers, or even the reflection question, so that the visit becomes a true ministry. It is to be remembered that ministers are not mere functionaries. As such, extraordinary ministers of Holy Communion bring not only the presence of Christ in the eucharistic species, but the presence of Christ in their very person by virtue of their baptism. So this book has been designed with that in mind, and it can be used to assist with making this a meaningful encounter and ministry.

In the hope of this Advent season, let us begin this Eucharist by acknowledging our sins, ever confident of the mercy and grace of God to restore and heal . . .

Prayer

May we watch with eyes set on the coming of the Lord, so that we may recognize Christ incarnate in those around us. With a profound sense of the sacred within the secular, we humbly pray for eyes with which to see. **Amen.**

Gospel   **Mark 13:33-37**

Jesus said to his disciples: "Be watchful! Be alert! You do not know when the time will come. It is like a man traveling abroad. He leaves home and places his servants in charge, each with his own work, and orders the gatekeeper to be on the watch. Watch, therefore; you do not know when the lord of the house is coming, whether in the evening, or at midnight, or at cockcrow, or in the morning. May he not come suddenly and find you sleeping. What I say to you, I say to all: 'Watch!'"

Brief Silence

For Reflection

We are plunged into the First Sunday of Advent with a reading from Mark 13. Jesus speaks about the coming end time, encouraging Peter, James, John, and Andrew (and us) to be watchful, to be prepared, and to recognize the signs of the times. The passage concludes this ominous chapter with the key word "watch" that occurs in each but one verse. "Watch" is an appropriate word with which to begin our Advent season. We are to be prepared for the Lord's coming, not knowing precisely when that will be. We, like the gatekeeper, keep watch in the evening, at midnight, at dawn, and in the morning. Like the early disciples, we know not when he comes, but that he is coming, perhaps not in an apocalyptic sense, but in the Christmas incarnation. That is, Jesus, the Word of God, comes to us in flesh and blood. Jesus is the incarnation of God, and he comes to us sacramentally in the Eucharist. We see that God is in our midst. The key word for this Sunday is "watch." But we may also say, "recognize."

✦ What has been my most difficult experience of watching—and how was I able to persevere to its fulfillment?

Brief Silence

Prayer

On this First Sunday of Advent we recall, "No ear has ever heard, no eye has ever seen" greater wonders than what God has done for us. You, O Lord, are the Potter and we are the clay, the work of your hands. Shape us in your ways of justice and mercy, form us in your peace, and craft us in your love. **Amen.**

With the faith and trust of Mary, Mother of the Word made flesh, let us place our hearts before God, confident of his mercy and forgiveness . . .

Prayer

May we, like Mary, hear your call and have the courage to respond by saying, "May it be done." May our free response give life to justice and liberation to the oppressed in our own time and place. We make these prayers to you in the name of your Son, Jesus the Christ. **Amen.**

Gospel **Luke 1:26-38**

The angel Gabriel was sent from God to a town of Galilee called Nazareth, to a virgin betrothed to a man named Joseph, of the house of David, and the virgin's name was Mary. And coming to her, he said, "Hail, full of grace! The Lord is with you." But she was greatly troubled at what was said and pondered what sort of greeting this might be. Then the angel said to her, "Do not be afraid, Mary, for you have found favor with God. Behold, you will conceive in your womb and bear a son, and you shall name him Jesus. He will be great and will be called Son of the Most High, and the Lord God will give him the throne of David his father, and he will rule over the house of Jacob forever, and of his Kingdom there will be no end." But Mary said to the angel, "How can this be, since I have no relations with a man?" And the angel said to her in reply, "The Holy Spirit will come upon you, and the power of the Most High will overshadow you. Therefore the child to be born will be called holy, the Son of God. And behold, Elizabeth, your relative, has also conceived a son in her old age, and this is the sixth month for her who was called barren; for nothing will be impossible for God." Mary said, "Behold, I am the handmaid of the Lord. May it be done to me according to your word." Then the angel departed from her.

Brief Silence

For Reflection

The gospel today tells us about Mary, full of grace, saying yes to God. By that yes, she cooperated with God for the salvation of humanity. For a moment, human salvation hung in the balance, dependent upon the "yes" from a human. Her affirmation of God's desire led to the birth of the Messiah and our eternal life. She was truly special, which is part of the reason the church commemorates her own conception. Heady ideas and a complex history of theology surround this solemnity. It's easy to get "lost in the weeds," so to speak; but, like Mary, let's keep our hearts focused on God and our "yes" to him. We ponder how much of God's plan of salvation is dependent upon human beings—not only Mary in her moment of "yes," but it is also dependent upon us. We first heard the gospel because somebody preached. Somebody said "yes" to God, which allows us to say "yes." Where are the moments in our daily lives where we need to say yes to what God has in store for us? It will likely not be a visit from an angel, but something more sublime. May we have eyes to see and ears to hear.

✦ What was the most important yes I have ever given? What causes me to be reluctant in giving my complete and trusting yes to the call of God?

Brief Silence

Prayer

In loving trust and faith, O God, your daughter Mary accepted your will for her to bring into the world your Son, the Messiah. May the prayers we offer to you today and our work to bring them to fulfillment bring the light and peace of Mary's child into our own time and place. We make these prayers to you in the name of your Son, Jesus the Christ. **Amen.**

God, our Shepherd and Father, has gathered us here. In hope, then, we pray for a broken people to be comforted with justice and peace in the land, so that as a result we may dwell with the Lord forever . . .

Prayer

God, you sent John the Baptist to prepare the way of the Lord and you continue to send prophets into our midst today. Give us ears to hear their words in the midst of our busy lives, which can be distracted by the noise of consumerism. **Amen.**

Gospel   **Mark 1:1-8**

The beginning of the Gospel of Jesus Christ the Son of God.

As it is written in Isaiah the prophet: / *Behold, I am sending my messenger ahead of you; / he will prepare your way. / A voice of one crying out in the desert: / "Prepare the way of the Lord, / make straight his paths."* / John the Baptist appeared in the desert proclaiming a baptism of repentance for the forgiveness of sins. People of the whole Judean countryside and all the inhabitants of Jerusalem were going out to him and were being baptized by him in the Jordan River as they acknowledged their sins. John was clothed in camel's hair, with a leather belt around his waist. He fed on locusts and wild honey. And this is what he proclaimed: "One mightier than I is coming after me. I am not worthy to stoop and loosen the thongs of his sandals. I have baptized you with water; he will baptize you with the Holy Spirit."

Brief Silence

For Reflection

With John the Baptist's unkempt appearance and fiery, apoca-lyptic preaching, he gathered crowds of those acknowledging their sins and seeking forgiveness. John the Baptist proclaims, "One mightier than I is coming after me." This person will baptize with the Holy Spirit. In these short verses the stage is set for Jesus. Mark has no infancy narrative such as Matthew or Luke would have it. There is no dramatic, cosmic prologue attuned to the open-ing words of Genesis as the Gospel of John would have it. Instead, Mark charges in, immediately quoting Scripture before introduc-ing John the Baptist. We readers are swept up in the story.

Perhaps it is appropriate that we read these opening verses on the Second Sunday of Advent with our busy lives, shopping lists, and details to which we must attend. The gospel, and especially its opening, seems to lend itself to our frenetic pace. Still there is the proclamation that something, someone, is coming. He is mightier than John the Baptist, mightier than our concerns for the season, mightier than our lists of things to get done. He will bap-tize with the Holy Spirit and our lives will never be the same.

✦ Who are the "prophets" among us who proclaim the presence of God in our midst?

Brief Silence

Prayer

May the glory of God be revealed in our work to make mercy, justice, and peace a reality in our own deserts and cities, and that by so doing we may see God's kingdom in our midst. **Amen.**

In a common hope based on God's limitless mercy, we pray for a broken people to be comforted with justice and peace in the land, so that we may dwell with the Lord forever . . .

Prayer

Lord God almighty, you sent your son Jesus into the world as the Lamb of God who takes away the sin of the world. In times of distress may we recall that the cosmic force of sin has been overcome by this same Son of yours. **Amen.**

Gospel   John 1:6-8, 19-28

A man named John was sent from God. He came for testimony, to testify to the light, so that all might believe through him. He was not the light, but came to testify to the light.

And this is the testimony of John. When the Jews from Jerusalem sent priests and Levites to him to ask him, "Who are you?" he admitted and did not deny it, but admitted, "I am not the Christ." So they asked him, "What are you then? Are you Elijah?" And he said, "I am not." "Are you the Prophet?" He answered, "No." So they said to him, "Who are you, so we can give an answer to those who sent us? What do you have to say for yourself?" He said: / "I am *the voice of one crying out in the desert, / 'make straight the way of the Lord,'* / as Isaiah the prophet said." Some Pharisees were also sent. They asked him, "Why then do you baptize if you are not the Christ or Elijah or the Prophet?" John answered them, "I baptize with water; but there is one among you whom you do not recognize, the one who is coming after me, whose sandal strap I am not worthy to untie." This happened in Bethany across the Jordan, where John was baptizing.

Brief Silence

For Reflection

On this "Gaudete" (Rejoice) Sunday, the Fourth Gospel states clearly and unequivocally that John was not the light, but was sent from God to testify to the light (John 1:8). John admits that he is not the Messiah; he is not Elijah; he is not even the prophet. His role is to cry out in the desert, "make straight the way of the Lord." We have heard these stories so often, and frequently from the Synoptic point of view. When we read the Fourth Gospel on its own terms we see that John says he baptizes with water. We might expect him to say, "but the one coming after me baptizes with the Holy Spirit" as we hear in the Synoptics. Instead, John says, "I baptize with water; / but there is *one among you whom you do not recognize.*" There is nothing in this gospel about Jesus baptizing with the Holy Spirit. Instead, Jesus is the Lamb of God who takes away the sin of the world. Once John testifies to the Lamb of God, John effectively disappears from the gospel. His role is basically confined to chapter 1 of the Fourth Gospel, and it consists in testifying to Jesus.

✦ How do I testify to the Lamb of God in our midst today?

Brief Silence

Prayer

Gracious God, may your Spirit come upon us to transform our lives and our world from barrenness to harvest, from sickness to wholeness, from division to completeness, from death to life. **Amen.**

As we await the dawning of the Lord, we prepare to celebrate these sacred mysteries by asking forgiveness for our sins and failings . . .

Prayer

Lord God, you deigned it worthy for your Son to be born of a woman. May Mary's "yes" inspire our own wholehearted response to your design for our lives. May her discipleship be a model for our own. **Amen.**

Gospel   Luke 1:26-38

The angel Gabriel was sent from God to a town of Galilee called Nazareth, to a virgin betrothed to a man named Joseph, of the house of David, and the virgin's name was Mary. And coming to her, he said, "Hail, full of grace! The Lord is with you." But she was greatly troubled at what was said and pondered what sort of greeting this might be. Then the angel said to her, "Do not be afraid, Mary, for you have found favor with God.

"Behold, you will conceive in your womb and bear a son, and you shall name him Jesus. He will be great and will be called Son of the Most High, and the Lord God will give him the throne of David his father, and he will rule over the house of Jacob forever, and of his kingdom there will be no end." But Mary said to the angel, "How can this be, since I have no relations with a man?" And the angel said to her in reply, "The Holy Spirit will come upon you, and the power of the Most High will overshadow you. Therefore the child to be born will be called holy, the Son of God. And behold, Elizabeth, your relative, has also conceived a son in her old age, and this is the sixth month for her who was called barren; for nothing will be impossible for God." Mary said,

"Behold, I am the handmaid of the Lord. May it be done to me according to your word." Then the angel departed from her.

Brief Silence

For Reflection

For the fourth and final Sunday of Advent we are brought back to the Gospel of Luke, and its beautiful story of the annunciation. Many church fathers spoke of how in that moment of the annunciation the entire plan of God hung in the balance, awaiting Mary's "yes." Human salvation, a free gift from God, depends upon human cooperation. In other words, God's gift is not forced but available to be freely accepted. Saint Bernard of Clairvaux wrote, "The angel awaits an answer; it is time for him to return to God who sent him. We too are waiting, O Lady, for your word of compassion." We then hear Mary's "fiat," the Latin rendering of "let it be done." And again, according to the church fathers, all heaven rejoices.

Though we celebrated the Annunciation on March 25, precisely nine months prior to Christmas, we read this gospel now, during the Fourth Sunday of Advent, because the incarnation was, in a certain way, dependent upon Mary's response. In Luke's story of the birth of Jesus, Mary plays a central role, setting the stage for centuries of theological reflection.

✦ When have my plans been "interrupted" or my perspective been changed by a moment of revelation?

Brief Silence

Prayer

O God, whose mercy is without limit and kindness is endless, hear our prayers as we eagerly await your coming into our homes and hearts in the birth of your Son, our Lord Jesus Christ. **Amen.**

Dear friends in Christ, rejoice! The Lord has come! He is the Light of God who dawns upon us; the child of Bethlehem born in simplicity. Let us open our hearts to welcome him with his reconciling peace and forgiveness . . .

Prayer

Lord God and Father of all, by sending your Son, you sent a peace the world did not know. Give us that peace now so that we may live our lives trusting in your providence and secure in your care for us. **Amen.**

Gospel   **Luke 2:1-14 (Mass at Midnight)**

In those days a decree went out from Caesar Augustus that the whole world should be enrolled. This was the first enrollment, when Quirinius was governor of Syria. So all went to be enrolled, each to his own town. And Joseph too went up from Galilee from the town of Nazareth to Judea, to the city of David that is called Bethlehem, because he was of the house and family of David, to be enrolled with Mary, his betrothed, who was with child. While they were there, the time came for her to have her child, and she gave birth to her firstborn son. She wrapped him in swaddling clothes and laid him in a manger, because there was no room for them in the inn.

Now there were shepherds in that region living in the fields and keeping the night watch over their flock. The angel of the Lord appeared to them and the glory of the Lord shone around them, and they were struck with great fear. The angel said to them, "Do not be afraid; for behold, I proclaim to you good news of great joy that will be for all the people. For today in the city of David a savior has been born for you who is Christ and Lord. And this will be a sign for you: you will find an infant wrapped in swaddling clothes and lying in a manger." And suddenly there was a multitude of the heavenly host with the angel, praising God and saying: / "Glory to God in the highest / and on earth peace to those on whom his favor rests."

Brief Silence

For Reflection

The gospel for the Mass at Midnight is Luke's familiar story of the birth of Jesus in a stable at Bethlehem during a census mandated by the Roman emperor. Augustus's long reign was hailed as the *pax Augusta*, a period of peace throughout the vast Roman world. But Rome's peace was not anything like "goodwill" as sung by the angels. It was a "peace" that was brutally enforced by intimidation and brutality. But the peace of Christmas is a very different kind of peace: it brings together heaven and earth, angels and mortals, shepherds and kings, society's dismissed outcasts and ruling elite. The *pax Christi* is not just the absence of strife but the presence of compassion and forgiveness; Christ's peace is built on justice for every human being, especially the vulnerable and the powerless. Christ's peace is the very foundation of the kingdom of God: peace that is not fearful passivity but loving perseverance that enables reconciliation and healing; peace that is not imposed but celebrated in mutual respect and generosity; peace that is not the province of the powerful but the responsibility of all "those on whom his favor rests."

✦ How can I further the *pax Christi* by my own actions in the world this Christmas season and throughout the New Year?

Brief Silence

Prayer

May our parish ministries proclaim the glad tidings of Christ's birth and may we all be instruments of Christ's peace and reconciliation in the world. Hear this prayer, O God, that we make this Christmas night/day in the name of our blessed hope, your Son and our Savior, Jesus Christ. **Amen.**

Let us prepare to celebrate these sacred mysteries by calling to mind our sins and failings, trusting in the mercy and forgiveness of God, the Father of us all . . .

Prayer

Lord God, you who calls prophetesses and prophets in every age, call forth the same in our own time. Give us eyes to see and ears to hear your words that they voice. **Amen.**

Gospel　　　　　　　　　　**Luke 2:22-40 (or Luke 2:22, 39-40)**

When the days were completed for their purification according to the law of Moses, they took him up to Jerusalem to present him to the Lord, just as it is written in the law of the Lord, *Every male that opens the womb shall be consecrated to the Lord,* and to offer the sacrifice of *a pair of turtledoves or two young pigeons,* in accordance with the dictate in the law of the Lord.

Now there was a man in Jerusalem whose name was Simeon. This man was righteous and devout, awaiting the consolation of Israel, and the Holy Spirit was upon him. It had been revealed to him by the Holy Spirit that he should not see death before he had seen the Christ of the Lord. He came in the Spirit into the temple; and when the parents brought in the child Jesus to perform the custom of the law in regard to him, he took him into his arms and blessed God, saying: / "Now, Master, you may let your servant go / in peace, according to your word, / for my eyes have seen your salvation, / which you prepared in sight of all the peoples, / a light for revelation to the Gentiles, / and glory for your people Israel." / The child's father and mother were amazed at what was said about him; and Simeon blessed them and said to Mary his mother, "Behold, this child is destined for the fall and rise of many in Israel, and to be a sign that will be contradicted—and you yourself a sword will pierce—so that the thoughts of many hearts may be revealed." There was also a prophetess, Anna, the daughter of

Phanuel, of the tribe of Asher. She was advanced in years, having lived seven years with her husband after her marriage, and then as a widow until she was eighty-four. She never left the temple, but worshiped night and day with fasting and prayer. And coming forward at that very time, she gave thanks to God and spoke about the child to all who were awaiting the redemption of Jerusalem.

When they had fulfilled all the prescriptions of the law of the Lord, they returned to Galilee, to their own town of Nazareth. The child grew and became strong, filled with wisdom; and the favor of God was upon him.

Brief Silence

For Reflection

Luke tells a rather unique story, often called "The Presentation of the Lord." While still an infant, Jesus is taken to the temple by his parents. Simeon's canticle begins with the words, "Now, Master, you may let your servant go / in peace." The promise to Simeon, that he would not see death until he had seen the Messiah of the Lord, is fulfilled. After Simeon exits the scene, the eighty-four-year-old widow prophetess Anna steps to the fore. Her worship is punctuated with fasting and prayer. She gives thanks to God and speaks about the child. It is significant that Luke includes this story. How many women prophets do we recall from the Old Testament? They are often men (Ezekiel, Isaiah, etc.). Yet, for Luke, not even Simeon is called a prophet. Instead Anna is a prophetess, foreshadowing the equality women enjoy in the ideal Christian life. This story, unique to Luke, reminds us of the equality of women and men, the relationship of the family, and the importance of human development as a place for God's favor.

✦ Who are the Simeons and Annas in my life and community?

Brief Silence

Prayer

Hear the prayers of your family gathered around your table, O Lord. As Jesus taught us to call you "Father," may we learn to respect and love one another as brothers and sisters. We offer these prayers to you in the name of your Son, Jesus, the Christ. **Amen.**

As the gift of a New Year dawns, let us come before the Lord in prayer for the peace and safety of all people . . .

Prayer

Christ of God, born of Mary, make your dwelling place among us so we may look upon the world in a new way, attentive to your incarnational presence. May our respect for the divine amidst the human reawaken in us a profound gratitude and humility for your sacred creation. **Amen.**

Gospel · Luke 2:16-21

The shepherds went in haste to Bethlehem and found Mary and Joseph, and the infant lying in the manger. When they saw this, they made known the message that had been told them about this child. All who heard it were amazed by what had been told them by the shepherds. And Mary kept all these things, reflecting on them in her heart. Then the shepherds returned, glorifying and praising God for all they had heard and seen, just as it had been told to them.

When eight days were completed for his circumcision, he was named Jesus, the name given him by the angel before he was conceived in the womb.

Brief Silence

For Reflection

Though this is New Year's Day in the secular calendar, according to the liturgical calendar this is the solemnity of Mary, the Holy Mother of God. In a sense we begin the New Year by reminding ourselves of some of the basics. How appropriate for Catholics that we begin the year by honoring Mary, and especially so that we refer to her as "Theotokos," "God-bearer," or more typically, "Mother of God." Like many Marian titles, this one says more about Jesus than it does about Mary. In the early church there were some who objected to such a title; they preferred to call Mary "Christotokos" or "Christ-bearer." Others who were perhaps more avant-garde used the more provocative "Theotokos" or "God-bearer." By this latter title, they meant that Jesus was the incarnation of God from the moment of his conception so that Mary could be called not merely bearer of the Christ, but bearer of God. For even in Mary's womb, Jesus was the incarnation of God. As such, Mary can be called the Mother of God. We begin the secular New Year with this reminder of a basic element of our faith, the incarnation. No resolutions are needed.

✦ How is the Mary of the gospels a wise, compelling companion for me on my journey through the year ahead?

Brief Silence

Prayer

Abba, "Father," hear the prayers we make for ourselves and for all members of our human family. With the faith and trust of Mary, may we make your gift of this New Year a time of reconciliation and grace, a season of peace and mercy for all your sons and daughters. We make these prayers in the name of Mary's child, your Son, Jesus the Christ. **Amen.**

The light of Christ has dawned, shattering the night of sin and despair. With humility and hope, let us begin our Eucharist celebrating the Epiphany of the Lord by seeking his forgiveness for our sins and failings . . .

Prayer

Lord of all, give to us your people, the coheirs to your promises, the faith shown by the magi. Give us the courage to follow the signs that lead to you, for it is our hope to worship you, the Emmanuel, "God with us." **Amen.**

Gospel   **Matt 2:1-12**

When Jesus was born in Bethlehem of Judea, in the days of King Herod, behold, magi from the east arrived in Jerusalem, saying, "Where is the newborn king of the Jews? We saw his star at its rising and have come to do him homage." When King Herod heard this, he was greatly troubled, and all Jerusalem with him. Assembling all the chief priests and the scribes of the people, he inquired of them where the Christ was to be born. They said to him, "In Bethlehem of Judea, for thus it has been written through the prophet: / *And you, Bethlehem, land of Judah, / are by no means least among the rulers of Judah; / since from you shall come a ruler, / who is to shepherd my people Israel."* / Then Herod called the magi secretly and ascertained from them the time of the star's appearance. He sent them to Bethlehem and said, "Go and search diligently for the child. When you have found him, bring me word, that I too may go and do him homage." After their audience with the king they set out. And behold, the star that they had seen at its rising preceded them, until it came and stopped over the place where the child was. They were overjoyed at seeing the star, and on entering the house they saw the child with Mary his mother. They prostrated themselves and did him homage. Then they opened their treasures and offered him gifts of gold, frankincense, and myrrh. And having been warned in a dream not to return to Herod, they departed for their country by another way.

Brief Silence

For Reflection

Today's gospel gives us the familiar story of the "visit of the magi." We have heard it so often that we may sometimes miss critical, and perhaps not so critical, elements in the story. In our own minds we have likely harmonized Matthew's nativity account with Luke's so that we place Luke's angels together with Matthew's magi in the crèche! But in Matthew's telling, there is no census that brings the family from Nazareth to Bethlehem, no manger, no animals, and no shepherds. Ultimately, the importance of what Matthew and Luke are telling us about the birth of Jesus rests not in details about where and how the family moved from Bethlehem to Nazareth, or whether Jesus was born in a home or a stable. Instead, Matthew is giving us a theological insight into the person of Jesus and the activity of God. The magi are not Jews. They are Gentiles. They worship Jesus. As such they prefigure the Gentile mission that the risen Jesus will inaugurate in the closing verses of this Gospel Matt 28:16-20). The Gentiles are coheirs with the Jews of the promises of God. We cannot limit God's mercy. It knows no bounds, and includes all!

✦ What "epiphanies" have I experienced in my life that have been most revealing and instructive?

Brief Silence

Prayer

Father, may your holy light illuminate the roads we walk on our journeys to you, as we seek to realize the hope of these prayers, prayers that we offer for all peoples in the name of your Christ. **Amen.**

Jesus is both Teacher and Word; he is the Anointed One, the Lamb of God given for all. Mindful of this, we humbly begin our celebration of these sacred mysteries by calling to mind our sins . . .

Prayer

Lord God, Lamb of God, you are the savior of the world. May we focus our attention on you as the source of all life and love, so that our relationships with one another may be a reflection of yours with the Father. **Amen.**

Gospel   John 1:35-42

John was standing with two of his disciples, and as he watched Jesus walk by, he said, "Behold, the Lamb of God." The two disciples heard what he said and followed Jesus. Jesus turned and saw them following him and said to them, "What are you looking for?" They said to him, "Rabbi"—which translated means Teacher—, "where are you staying?" He said to them, "Come, and you will see." So they went and saw where Jesus was staying, and they stayed with him that day. It was about four in the afternoon. Andrew, the brother of Simon Peter, was one of the two who heard John and followed Jesus. He first found his own brother Simon and told him, "We have found the Messiah"—which is translated Christ. Then he brought him to Jesus. Jesus looked at him and said, "You are Simon the son of John; you will be called Cephas"—which is translated Peter.

Brief Silence

For Reflection

In Ordinary Time it might be surprising to read from the Gospel of John, the author of which is also known as "The Theologian." In today's story we have the calling of the first disciples, only one of whom is named: Andrew the brother of Simon Peter. Andrew and the unnamed disciple evangelize Simon, Andrew's brother, by saying they have found the Messiah. They bring Simon to Jesus. And before Simon can say a word, Jesus names him "Cephas," the Aramaic term for "Rock," translated into Greek as "Petros," from which we get the name "Peter." This story of Jesus naming Simon "Peter" is much different than that in the Synoptics, where Jesus names him "Peter" only after Simon confesses Jesus as the Messiah (Matt 16:16; Mark 8:29; Luke 9:20). The Gospel of John, with its intense emphasis on Jesus, does not allow the possibility of Simon's name change to be associated with his confession, or absolutely anything else Simon has done. Simon merely hears the news and comes to meet Jesus. So we see clearly Johannine theology with its overriding emphasis on Jesus. For this reason and many others the author of this gospel has been named "The Theologian."

✦ Like "The Theologian," is my emphasis on Jesus and him alone?

Brief Silence

Prayer

Hear, O Lord, these prayers we offer. May your Spirit dwelling within us and in the midst of this community help us to make the kingdom of God a reality in our time. We ask this in the name of Jesus, your Christ. **Amen.**

The Lord God Almighty shows the humble his way. He guides us to justice and remembers us when we stray. As we prepare to celebrate this Eucharist, in the certain hope of God's forgiveness, we call to mind our sins and failings . . .

Prayer

Good and gracious God, you call us and we respond with enthusiasm. But often the scars we encounter on the journey can take their toll. Rekindle in us the same spirit of enthusiasm that animated the response of the first disciples. **Amen.**

Gospel   Mark 1:14-20

After John had been arrested, Jesus came to Galilee proclaiming the gospel of God: "This is the time of fulfillment. The kingdom of God is at hand. Repent, and believe in the gospel."

As he passed by the Sea of Galilee, he saw Simon and his brother Andrew casting their nets into the sea; they were fishermen. Jesus said to them, "Come after me, and I will make you fishers of men." Then they abandoned their nets and followed him. He walked along a little farther and saw James, the son of Zebedee, and his brother John. They too were in a boat mending their nets. Then he called them. So they left their father Zebedee in the boat along with the hired men and followed him.

Brief Silence

For Reflection

In today's story we hear something of the preaching of Jesus, which to a certain degree echoed that of John the Baptist. Jesus' preaching will be developed and expanded throughout the Gospel of Mark, but at this early stage it is centered around the twofold command, "Repent, and believe." The story is certainly idealized for dramatic effect; we only need to look at last week's Gospel of John to see another version of Andrew and Peter being called by Jesus. But what is Mark telling us by narrating the story the way he does? Certainly that these first disciples left everything in a single-minded pursuit of Jesus. As such, they represent the ideal. Still, as we will learn throughout this gospel, the disciples did not often live up to that ideal. And perhaps this is another lesson of Mark's story. Our beginnings can be filled with such idealism, promise, and pure-hearted devotion. Only later will "reality" begin to sink in and our failings and shortcomings become apparent, as they no doubt will with the disciples.

✦ Is the initial joy and devotion of giving my life to the Gospel still animating me today? Why or why not?

Brief Silence

Prayer

Timeless and eternal God, help us to realize that your gift of time is not the end or limit of this life but the pathway to the complete and perfect life of the risen One, in whose name we pray. **Amen.**

Jesus reconciles us to God and to one another by driving out the unclean spirits of sin that possess us. We therefore begin our celebration of these sacred mysteries by confessing our failings and sins, confident of God's mercy and grace . . .

Prayer

God of justice, you sent your Son into the world and in so doing he confronted evil and injustice. Send us as disciples of your Son to confront the evil and injustice we encounter so that we might be participants in building your kingdom on earth. **Amen.**

Gospel   Mark 1:21-28

Then they came to Capernaum, and on the sabbath Jesus entered the synagogue and taught. The people were astonished at his teaching, for he taught them as one having authority and not as the scribes. In their synagogue was a man with an unclean spirit; he cried out, "What have you to do with us, Jesus of Nazareth? Have you come to destroy us? I know who you are—the Holy One of God!" Jesus rebuked him and said, "Quiet! Come out of him!" The unclean spirit convulsed him and with a loud cry came out of him. All were amazed and asked one another, "What is this? A new teaching with authority. He commands even the unclean spirits and they obey him." His fame spread everywhere throughout the whole region of Galilee.

Brief Silence

For Reflection

Having called his first four disciples, Jesus goes to the village of Capernaum on the Sea of Galilee, where he begins to teach in the synagogue. He is confronted by evil, a man with an unclean spirit. As we have it in this story, Jesus commands the evil spirit to come out of the man, and it obeys, though not without dramatic theatrics. The assembled people were understandably amazed. And, not surprisingly, Jesus' reputation spread. It is significant that the disciples were with Jesus during this encounter. We see that no sooner had the disciples been called by Jesus to be his followers than did they encounter evil. The disciples are in relationship with Jesus, and as such they witness the opposition he faces. Later they will encounter similar opposition. Even though the gospel does not tell the story, we, like those in Mark's community, know that many of Jesus' disciples lost their lives too in confrontations with evil. The gospel reminds us that we too will confront evil if we are true disciples of Jesus. We are to be doers of the word and not merely those who listen.

✦ When and how do I confront evil or injustice in the world?

Brief Silence

Prayer

Father of mercy, hear our prayers and instill in us your Spirit so that, in imitating your Son's humble generosity and reconciling peace, we may bring these prayers to reality. In Jesus' name, we pray. **Amen.**

Jesus lifts up the sinner and grasps the failing. With trust in him, let us open our hearts to the healing mercy of God by humbly acknowledging our sins and failings . . .

Prayer

Lord Jesus, you came among us healing the sick and comforting the afflicted. Make us instruments of your healing and comforting ministry in our own lives, so that we might be your followers in word and in deed. **Amen.**

Gospel   Mark 1:29-39

On leaving the synagogue Jesus entered the house of Simon and Andrew with James and John. Simon's mother-in-law lay sick with a fever. They immediately told him about her. He approached, grasped her hand, and helped her up. Then the fever left her and she waited on them.

When it was evening, after sunset, they brought to him all who were ill or possessed by demons. The whole town was gathered at the door. He cured many who were sick with various diseases, and he drove out many demons, not permitting them to speak because they knew him.

Rising very early before dawn, he left and went off to a deserted place, where he prayed. Simon and those who were with him pursued him and on finding him said, "Everyone is looking for you." He told them, "Let us go on to the nearby villages that I may preach there also. For this purpose have I come." So he went into their synagogues, preaching and driving out demons throughout the whole of Galilee.

Brief Silence

For Reflection

The action in today's gospel begins in Capernaum, where Jesus has been preaching in the synagogue. He and his new disciples (for they were called by Jesus only a few verses earlier) go to the house of the brothers Simon and Andrew. There Simon's mother-in-law is healed. A few things are clear: Simon (Peter) had a wife; and the extended family, including at least his brother and his mother-in-law, lived under the same roof. This particular home must have been a welcoming place. Not only was it the location of such an extended family, but James and John were also with them that day. And by evening it seemed the entire town was at the door! Jesus cured many of the townspeople before leaving early the next day.

The action and excitement covered in this brief period is palpable. In one sense it covers only twenty-four hours before concluding with a sentence that says he went throughout the whole of Galilea preaching and driving out demons. Jesus has a purpose and his followers are witness to it. Excitement fills the air with the wonders Jesus does.

✦ Do I have a "deserted place" in my life where or when I am alone with God?

Brief Silence

Prayer

O Lord, you have walked among us; you know our pain and our brokenness. May these prayers we offer be the beginning of the mending of our relationships with one another and the healing of our hearts in your hope and peace. In Jesus' name, we pray. **Amen.**

God is the source of all that is good. In him we are healed and made whole. Aware of our shortcomings and in preparation to celebrate these sacred mysteries, we call to mind our sins, trusting in God's goodness . . .

Prayer

Lord Jesus, you came into the world to cure the sick and restore communities to wholeness. Give us the same spirit that animated your ministry so that we may be agents of healing and inclusion in our own places this day. **Amen.**

Gospel   Mark 1:40-45

A leper came to Jesus and kneeling down begged him and said, "If you wish, you can make me clean." Moved with pity, he stretched out his hand, touched him, and said to him, "I do will it. Be made clean." The leprosy left him immediately, and he was made clean. Then, warning him sternly, he dismissed him at once.

He said to him, "See that you tell no one anything, but go, show yourself to the priest and offer for your cleansing what Moses prescribed; that will be proof for them."

The man went away and began to publicize the whole matter. He spread the report abroad so that it was impossible for Jesus to enter a town openly. He remained outside in deserted places, and people kept coming to him from everywhere.

Brief Silence

For Reflection

Though in the story today our English Bibles refer to the person cured as a "leper," the term means anyone with a skin disease. Those with such an affliction had to cry out, "unclean, unclean" before approaching others (Lev 13:45-46). They also had to live apart from the community for as long as the infection lasted. So the healing performed by Jesus is not merely a healing of the skin disease, though it is certainly that. But once cured, the man will be brought back into community. Jesus' ministry was about inclusion. He ministered to those on the margins, or even to those outside of the community, like this person with a skin disease; and Jesus made them whole. Once whole, the excluded persons could be welcomed back.

Whom do we see excluded today? If we want to be like Jesus we can find those on the margins and bring them into the fold. We may not have the power to heal physical ailments, but we can certainly reach out to the marginalized and draw them close.

✦ Have I ever felt like a "leper"—segregated, isolated, estranged, misunderstood?

Brief Silence

Prayer

Hear our prayers, O God, for all the family of humankind. Mend our broken relationships with one another; heal us of the leprosy of selfishness and injustice; make us clean and whole in your love and compassion. We offer these prayers in the name of Jesus, the healing Christ. **Amen.**

As we begin this Lenten season, let us take stock of our lives and acknowledge the times we have failed to live up to our Christian ideals . . .

Prayer

Lord God Almighty, you call us in this Lenten season to reexamine our lives in the light of your Christ. Shine that light brightly so that our shortcomings are revealed and thus we may amend ourselves for your service. **Amen.**

Gospel   **Matt 6:1-6, 16-18**

Jesus said to his disciples: "Take care not to perform righteous deeds in order that people may see them; otherwise, you will have no recompense from your heavenly Father. When you give alms, do not blow a trumpet before you, as the hypocrites do in the synagogues and in the streets to win the praise of others. Amen, I say to you, they have received their reward. But when you give alms, do not let your left hand know what your right is doing, so that your almsgiving may be secret. And your Father who sees in secret will repay you.

"When you pray, do not be like the hypocrites, who love to stand and pray in the synagogues and on street corners so that others may see them. Amen, I say to you, they have received their reward. But when you pray, go to your inner room, close the door, and pray to your Father in secret. And your Father who sees in secret will repay you.

"When you fast, do not look gloomy like the hypocrites. They neglect their appearance, so that they may appear to others to be fasting. Amen, I say to you, they have received their reward. But when you fast, anoint your head and wash your face, so that you may not appear to be fasting, except to your Father who is hidden. And your Father who sees what is hidden will repay you."

Brief Silence

For Reflection

Today we seem to do the opposite of the Gospel injunction, wearing ashes, by which others see we have been to Mass. Of course, that isn't the purpose of the ashes, but that's the result. The ashes on our foreheads mark us as Mass-goers on this unique day. But what if we went to Mass today only to wash off the ashes immediately afterwards? What would people think if they did not see ashes on our foreheads? Would they wonder if we had been to Mass? Might we be judged as shirking a Catholic ritual, though certainly not a holy day of obligation?

Jesus reminded his followers, and he therefore reminds us, that our good deeds, prayers, almsgiving, and fasting ought to be done in secret. In so doing there will be no admiration from others. There will be no acclaim. There will be no external attention. Instead, one's heavenly Father is the audience, nobody else. God alone knows our hearts and our actions. We do not need to justify ourselves before anyone but God.

✦ How can I ensure that my Lenten practices are done not for show, but for God?

Brief Silence

Prayer

Merciful God, look upon us as we enter these forty days of Lent, bearing on our heads the marks of ashes. May our fasting be a hunger for justice; may our alms be the means of peace and reconciliation; may our prayers be the hopes we are prepared to work and sacrifice for. In Jesus' name, we pray. **Amen.**

Called by the Spirit to the Lenten desert with Christ, let us ask for the mercy of God for our sins . . .

Prayer

Lord God, you called Jesus into the desert where he faced temptation. Give us the same strength you gave to your Son in those moments when we are tempted so we may emerge to proclaim your kingdom. **Amen.**

Gospel   Mark 1:12-15

The Spirit drove Jesus out into the desert, and he remained in the desert for forty days, tempted by Satan. He was among wild beasts, and the angels ministered to him.

After John had been arrested, Jesus came to Galilee proclaiming the gospel of God: "This is the time of fulfillment. The kingdom of God is at hand. Repent, and believe in the gospel."

Brief Silence

For Reflection

In the desert, Jesus faces something much more profound than temptation around a New Year's resolution or an intention to exercise daily. This desert is a place of no consolation, no respite, and no refreshment. The experience of knowing he is God's Son gives way to isolation and solitude in a harsh environment. Mark does not tell us much about this period, unlike Luke, for example, with the many scenes of Jesus conversing with Satan. Mark is intent to tell us in sparse text, without wasting a word, that Jesus was tempted by Satan. Jesus was fully human and experienced temptation as we do.

As Jesus was tempted we too will be tempted. Perhaps even our profound experience of faith and trust in God is tested. But after this period of testing Jesus returns to Galilee, his home, and proclaims the Gospel. In this he is a model for us, who will not live without temptation. We might have an experience of desolation that God is not with us in our trials. But like Jesus we can undergo this experience and emerge stronger, with the courage to proclaim the Gospel.

✦ When was a time I emerged from "the desert"?

Brief Silence

Prayer

Hear the prayers we offer to you, O Lord. During these holy days of Lent, may we dedicate ourselves to the work of making these prayers a reality. We ask these things of you in the name of Jesus, our Redeemer. **Amen.**

Confident of God's constant mercy, let us begin our prayer by calling to mind our sins . . .

Prayer

Lord Jesus Christ, you fulfill the Law and Prophets, you are the resurrection and the life. Give us a share in your eternal life, so that, living lives of righteousness on earth, we may live in your reign forever in heaven. **Amen.**

Gospel   **Mark 9:2-10**

Jesus took Peter, James, and John and led them up a high mountain apart by themselves. And he was transfigured before them, and his clothes became dazzling white, such as no fuller on earth could bleach them. Then Elijah appeared to them along with Moses, and they were conversing with Jesus. Then Peter said to Jesus in reply, "Rabbi, it is good that we are here! Let us make three tents: one for you, one for Moses, and one for Elijah." He hardly knew what to say, they were so terrified. Then a cloud came, casting a shadow over them; from the cloud came a voice, "This is my beloved Son. Listen to him." Suddenly, looking around, they no longer saw anyone but Jesus alone with them.

As they were coming down from the mountain, he charged them not to relate what they had seen to anyone, except when the Son of Man had risen from the dead. So they kept the matter to themselves, questioning what rising from the dead meant.

Brief Silence

For Reflection

With the story of the transfiguration, the language of this encounter is steeped in symbolism, beginning with the mountain itself, but including the white garments, the cloud, the voice from heaven, and the figures alongside Jesus. The garments Jesus wears are turned "dazzling white." The symbolism should be clear. He is pure. Moses and Elijah, appearing alongside Jesus, represent the Law and the Prophets. Jesus fulfills both; his ministry is in continuity with Moses and Elijah. He is not doing anything contrary to either.

Rather than rest in the moment, and simply take in the wonderment of it all, Peter breaks into the scene with an idea to make three tents, which would be places of worship, commemorating this event. But no sooner had he voiced this proposal than God himself, the voice from heaven, speaks in a way reminiscent of Jesus' baptism: "You are my beloved Son; with you I am well pleased" (Mark 1:11). Now the three disciples, not present at Jesus' baptism, hear the voice too. And with that, the episode ends. The three disciples are left alone with Jesus to come down from the mountain, struggling to understand what this experience and Jesus' own admonition meant.

✦ What has been a mountaintop experience for me? And did I struggle to understand its meaning?

Brief Silence

Prayer

Father, hear the prayers we make before you. May your Spirit of compassion and peace "transfigure" us and our world into the image of Jesus, the risen Christ, in whose name we offer these prayers. **Amen.**

God has invited us to this house of prayer to offer and receive the gift of the Eucharist. Let us begin by placing our hearts in God's peace and asking his forgiveness for our sins and failings . . .

Prayer

Lord God, your son Jesus taught us that relationships and care for the other are integral aspects of true worship of you. May we work to alleviate suffering, homelessness, hunger, and poverty in our world, motivated by the faith and teachings of your Son. **Amen.**

Gospel   **John 2:13-25**

Since the Passover of the Jews was near, Jesus went up to Jerusalem. He found in the temple area those who sold oxen, sheep, and doves, as well as the money changers seated there. He made a whip out of cords and drove them all out of the temple area, with the sheep and oxen, and spilled the coins of the money changers and overturned their tables, and to those who sold doves he said, "Take these out of here, and stop making my Father's house a marketplace." His disciples recalled the words of Scripture, *Zeal for your house will consume me.* At this the Jews answered and said to him, "What sign can you show us for doing this?" Jesus answered and said to them, "Destroy this temple and in three days I will raise it up." The Jews said, "This temple has been under construction for forty-six years, and you will raise it up in three days?" But he was speaking about the temple of his body. Therefore, when he was raised from the dead, his disciples remembered that he had said this, and they came to believe the Scripture and the word Jesus had spoken.

While he was in Jerusalem for the feast of Passover, many began to believe in his name when they saw the signs he was doing. But Jesus would not trust himself to them because he knew them all, and did not need anyone to testify about human nature. He himself understood it well.

Brief Silence

For Reflection

The gospel tells us something today that we can often overlook. The temple is not only the physical place in Jerusalem, but metaphorically it is Jesus' very self. By extension, the human body, the human self is a place of God's presence. True worship therefore becomes how we treat ourselves, and how we treat the other. But treating another kindly, patiently, and with love can be much more difficult than dropping a few dollars in the basket or writing a check. Our relationship with God is dependent upon how we treat the other, who is a dwelling place of God in our midst. It can be difficult to die to our preconceived notions of God, to let go of the idea of an accountant God who takes stock of each and every sacrifice, ensuring it is without blemish. Instead, Jesus invites us to a relationship with God based on Jesus himself, the enfleshment of God. If Jesus is the incarnation of God, if humanity is a dwelling place for the divinity, then proper worship becomes how we treat our neighbor.

✦ In what ways does my parish realize Jesus' vision of "my Father's house" in today's gospel?

Brief Silence

Prayer

We come before you, O God, with open and humble hearts. Give us the vision to seek you in all things, so that our lives may be made complete in your joy and made whole in your compassionate love. Hear these prayers we ask of you in the name of Jesus, our Redeemer. **Amen.**

God is rich in mercy and compassion. As we prepare to celebrate these sacred mysteries, we ask for his forgiveness for our sins and failings . . .

Prayer

Good and gracious God, you raise the dead to new life. The resurrection of your Son is your promise for our own eternal life. May the joy of that Easter morning inform our lives all year round. **Amen.**

Gospel   **John 3:14-21**

Jesus said to Nicodemus: "Just as Moses lifted up the serpent in the desert, so must the Son of Man be lifted up, so that everyone who believes in him may have eternal life."

For God so loved the world that he gave his only Son, so that everyone who believes in him might not perish but might have eternal life. For God did not send his Son into the world to condemn the world, but that the world might be saved through him. Whoever believes in him will not be condemned, but whoever does not believe has already been condemned, because he has not believed in the name of the only Son of God. And this is the verdict, that the light came into the world, but people preferred darkness to light, because their works were evil. For everyone who does wicked things hates the light and does not come toward the light, so that his works might not be exposed. But whoever lives the truth comes to the light, so that his works may be clearly seen as done in God.

Brief Silence

For Reflection

This Fourth Sunday of Lent is traditionally called "*Laetare*" Sunday, from the Latin meaning "to rejoice" or "to be joyful." The term comes from the Introit (Isa 66:10). It might seem odd to "rejoice" in Lent, but that exhortation is a reminder, or rather a foreshadowing, of Easter. It is as though Easter itself is breaking into the Lenten season this Sunday.

The passage that many use to sum up the gospel is simply this: "For God so loved the world that he gave his only Son." The profundity of this statement can be lost by its pithiness. We proclaim a God of love, not a God of condemnation. And this love results in God sending his only Son, Jesus. The starting point of our theology is, then, love.

Though many today and throughout history seem to prefer a God of judgment, a God of condemnation, today we are reminded that our God is love. And God's love is eternal, expressed in a never-ending life he wants for each of us, where the relationships and bonds we create in this life are never broken. On this Laetare Sunday, where we read John 3:16, may our coming Easter joy be complete in this Lenten season.

✦ How does the joy of Easter inform my life today?

Brief Silence

Prayer

May our prayers be the stones of our temple of praise to you, O Lord; may our acts of compassion and selflessness build us into the Body of Christ, your beloved Son, in whose name we offer these prayers. **Amen.**

Confident of the never failing mercy of God, we begin our celebration of the Eucharist by calling to mind our sins, for we join our prayers with those of the obedient Christ Jesus . . .

Prayer

God, Father of all, you sent your Son into the world to die for our sins, and you raised him to new life. Give us the ability to see the new life that comes from death, hope from tragedy, peace and strength from sorrow and loss. **Amen.**

Gospel   John 12:20-33

Some Greeks who had come to worship at the Passover Feast came to Philip, who was from Bethsaida in Galilee, and asked him, "Sir, we would like to see Jesus." Philip went and told Andrew; then Andrew and Philip went and told Jesus. Jesus answered them, "The hour has come for the Son of Man to be glorified. Amen, amen, I say to you, unless a grain of wheat falls to the ground and dies, it remains just a grain of wheat; but if it dies, it produces much fruit. Whoever loves his life loses it, and whoever hates his life in this world will preserve it for eternal life. Whoever serves me must follow me, and where I am, there also will my servant be. The Father will honor whoever serves me.

"I am troubled now. Yet what should I say? 'Father, save me from this hour'? But it was for this purpose that I came to this hour. Father, glorify your name." Then a voice came from heaven, "I have glorified it and will glorify it again." The crowd there heard it and said it was thunder; but others said, "An angel has spoken to him." Jesus answered and said, "This voice did not come for my sake but for yours. Now is the time of judgment on this world; now the ruler of this world will be driven out. And when I am lifted up from the earth, I will draw everyone to myself." He said this indicating the kind of death he would die.

Brief Silence

For Reflection

In this Lenten Sunday preceding Palm Sunday we share a sense of impending doom. But we are also reminded of the necessity of death for something to bear fruit. If the seed stays on the countertop, it will never bear fruit. But once "dead" and planted in the ground, the seed produces. The paschal mystery is presented for us in a simple, agrarian, even if scientifically outdated, image. It's true that the ancients did not have the knowledge about biology that we have today. Upon hearing the metaphor of a seed dying to produce much fruit, many in a modern audience might critique the analogy. For we know that a seed does not truly die, but the soil, moisture, and light cause an organic change. Still we do not want to lose the message in spite of the metaphor. Only by his death will Jesus' ministry truly bear fruit. That is the necessary next step. His death is necessary because this is the purpose for which Jesus came. There is no sidestepping or dodging this inevitable end, which is ratified by a voice from heaven. The end is near.

✦ How have I experienced the dying and the harvest of the grain of wheat in my life?

Brief Silence

Prayer

God of life, Source of love, accept the offering of our prayers. Bless us always with the hope of the grain of wheat, so that we may seek to die to ourselves for the sake of others, and one day rise to the new life of the eternal springtime of your Son, our Lord and risen Savior, Jesus Christ. **Amen.**

Our Holy Week journey with Jesus begins with his entry into Jerusalem to shouts of "Hosanna" and the joyful waving of palm branches. In the days ahead, the joy of this moment will be darkened by betrayal and death. Let us begin our Palm Sunday liturgy by placing our hearts in the love of God, who, in his Son, takes up the cross in order to bring us to Easter resurrection . . .

Prayer

Lord God Almighty, you were with Jesus on the cross in the final moments before his death. Give us the assurance that you are with us always, even in our darkest hour, when we do not feel your presence. **Amen.**

Gospel   Mark 15:1-39 (or Mark 14:1–15:47)

As soon as morning came, the chief priests with the elders and the scribes, that is, the whole Sanhedrin held a council. They bound Jesus, led him away, and handed him over to Pilate. Pilate questioned him, "Are you the king of the Jews?" He said to him in reply, "You say so." The chief priests accused him of many things. Again Pilate questioned him, "Have you no answer? See how many things they accuse you of." Jesus gave him no further answer, so that Pilate was amazed.

Now on the occasion of the feast he used to release to them one prisoner whom they requested. A man called Barabbas was then in prison along with the rebels who had committed murder in a rebellion. The crowd came forward and began to ask him to do for them as he was accustomed. Pilate answered, "Do you want me to release to you the king of the Jews?" For he knew that it was out of envy that the chief priests had handed him over. But the chief priests stirred up the crowd to have him release Barabbas for them instead. Pilate again said to them in reply, "Then what do you want me to do with the man you call the king of the Jews?" They shouted again, "Crucify him." Pilate said to them, "Why? What evil has he done?" They only shouted the louder, "Crucify him." So Pilate, wishing to satisfy the crowd, released Barabbas to them and, after he had Jesus scourged, handed him over to be crucified.

The soldiers led him away inside the palace, that is, the praetorium, and assembled the whole cohort. They clothed him in purple and, weaving a crown of thorns, placed it on him. They began to salute him with, "Hail, King of the Jews!" and kept striking his head with a reed and spitting upon him. They knelt before him in homage. And when they had mocked him, they stripped him of the purple cloak, dressed him in his own clothes, and led him out to crucify him.

They pressed into service a passer-by, Simon, a Cyrenian, who was coming in from the country, the father of Alexander and Rufus, to carry his cross.

They brought him to the place of Golgotha—which is translated Place of the Skull—. They gave him wine drugged with myrrh, but he did not take it. Then they crucified him and divided his garments by casting lots for them to see what each should take. It was nine o'clock in the morning when they crucified him. The inscription of the charge against him read, "The King of the Jews." With him they crucified two revolutionaries, one on his right and one on his left. Those passing by reviled him, shaking their heads and saying, "Aha! You who would destroy the temple and rebuild it in three days, save yourself by coming down from the cross." Likewise the chief priests, with the scribes, mocked him among themselves and said, "He saved others; he cannot save himself. Let the Christ, the King of Israel, come down now from the cross that we may see and believe." Those who were crucified with him also kept abusing him.

At noon darkness came over the whole land until three in the afternoon. And at three o'clock Jesus cried out in a loud voice, *"Eloi, Eloi, lema sabachthani?"* which is translated, "My God, my God, why have you forsaken me?" Some of the bystanders who heard it said, "Look, he is calling Elijah." One of them ran, soaked a sponge with wine, put it on a reed and gave it to him to drink saying, "Wait, let us see if Elijah comes to take him down." Jesus gave a loud cry and breathed his last.

The veil of the sanctuary was torn in two from top to bottom. When the centurion who stood facing him saw how he breathed his last he said, "Truly this man was the Son of God!"

Brief Silence

For Reflection

Jesus did not meet the expectations of the crowd, or even his disciples, they turned and fled. One disciple ran so fast he ran out of his clothes (Mark 14:51-52)! Peter, of course, denied he even knew Jesus. The crowd chose to have an insurrectionist released to them rather than Jesus. By the time Jesus was on the cross the only remaining friends were some women and Joseph of Arimathea. They stand in contrast to the behavior of the disciples who denied Jesus, or simply fled the scene.

The entire passion narrative in Mark shows the confusion, bewilderment, and misunderstanding that punctuated the horrific scene of Jesus' crucifixion. The crowds believe Jesus is calling for Elijah, the chief priests and scribes mock Jesus as one who cannot save himself, Pilate acquiesces to the crowd's demands and participates in a miscarriage of justice. The centurion alone (a Gentile) is the one to face the crucified after death and proclaim, "Truly this man was the Son of God!" (Mark 15:39). To be the Christ, the Son of God, necessarily means suffering and death. Rather than a political military leader commanding armies in a revolution, Jesus is the crucified Son of God, Messiah. God's plans are not our own.

✦ When have I felt abandoned by God, but discovered him again in my life?

Brief Silence

Prayer

Father of endless love and compassion, hear the prayers of your family gathered around your altar. May we imitate your Son by taking up our crosses with joyful obedience, seeking your justice in all things; may we embrace his example of loving humility, praising you in the compassionate care we extend to one another. **Amen.**

Tonight Jesus gives his commandment to wash each other's feet in a spirit of humility and service to one another. Let us begin this evening's Mass of the Lord's Supper by placing our hearts in the presence of God, seeking his mercy as we acknowledge our failure to realize Jesus' commandment to love one another as he has loved us . . .

Prayer

Lord Jesus, you who are Master bent down and washed the feet of your disciples. In so doing you gave us an example for how we are to behave. When our own priorities occupy our thoughts, give us the spirit of self-giving service so that we may imitate you and continue your ministry in the world today. **Amen.**

Gospel   John 13:1-15

Before the feast of Passover, Jesus knew that his hour had come to pass from this world to the Father. He loved his own in the world and he loved them to the end. The devil had already induced Judas, son of Simon the Iscariot, to hand him over. So, during supper, fully aware that the Father had put everything into his power and that he had come from God and was returning to God, he rose from supper and took off his outer garments. He took a towel and tied it around his waist. Then he poured water into a basin and began to wash the disciples' feet and dry them with the towel around his waist. He came to Simon Peter, who said to him, "Master, are you going to wash my feet?" Jesus answered and said to him, "What I am doing, you do not understand now, but you will understand later." Peter said to him, "You will never wash my feet." Jesus answered him, "Unless I wash you, you will have no inheritance with me." Simon Peter said to him, "Master, then not only my feet, but my hands and head as well." Jesus said to him, "Whoever has bathed has no need except to have his feet washed, for he is clean all over; so you are clean, but not all." For he knew who would betray him; for this reason, he said, "Not all of you are clean."

So when he had washed their feet and put his garments back on and reclined at table again, he said to them, "Do you realize what I have done for you? You call me 'teacher' and 'master,' and rightly so, for indeed I am. If I, therefore, the master and teacher, have washed your feet, you ought to wash one another's feet. I have given you a model to follow, so that as I have done for you, you should also do."

Brief Silence

For Reflection

The church gives us this reading from the Gospel of John on Holy Thursday to remind us of the Christian call to imitate the master who served. For the Christian, service is required. It is not something we do only when we feel so moved. Rather, it is a fundamental and constitutive element of our identity. We act this way, in service, because of the example Jesus himself gave us. Of course, if his life and death were not example enough, we have this further action on his part during the Last Supper. So in addition to healing the sick, curing the lame, making the blind see, we have one further example par excellence. Jesus bent down, and washed the feet of his disciples, even though they called him "Master." Such an example reverberates through the centuries. Jesus reminds us that to be the master is to be the servant. In so doing, Jesus overturns cultural and societal norms. This action is not to be a "once-off," or "one-and-done" kind of service for show, so we can be admired for how much we serve. Instead, this is to be our way of being.

✦ How can I be "Eucharist" to others?

Brief Silence

Prayer

Hear the prayers we offer you this night, O God, as we gather to celebrate your Son's Passover. By your grace, make us bread for one another and "footwashers" in the spirit of your Son, our Lord Jesus Christ, in whose name we pray. **Amen.**

On this Easter morning, God raises us up from the tombs of our sins and failings. In the risen Christ, we are recreated in the love of God. And so, with humility and joy, let us begin our Easter Eucharist by asking God's forgiveness and peace . . .

Prayer

Lord God, you raised Jesus from the dead. Give us the faith of the Beloved Disciple, who discerned meaning from the empty tomb and believed in the resurrection. **Amen.**

Gospel   John 20:1-9

On the first day of the week, Mary of Magdala came to the tomb early in the morning, while it was still dark, and saw the stone removed from the tomb. So she ran and went to Simon Peter and to the other disciple whom Jesus loved, and told them, "They have taken the Lord from the tomb, and we don't know where they put him." So Peter and the other disciple went out and came to the tomb. They both ran, but the other disciple ran faster than Peter and arrived at the tomb first; he bent down and saw the burial cloths there, but did not go in. When Simon Peter arrived after him, he went into the tomb and saw the burial cloths there, and the cloth that had covered his head, not with the burial cloths but rolled up in a separate place. Then the other disciple also went in, the one who had arrived at the tomb first, and he saw and believed. For they did not yet understand the Scripture that he had to rise from the dead.

Brief Silence

For Reflection

Easter morning must have been a confusing, even frightening, time. Jesus had just been killed by the state, an imperial occupying power. Most of the disciples had scattered. In this as in the other gospel accounts, the first indications of Jesus' resurrection were the discovery of the empty tomb. The appearances of the risen Jesus came later. Initially the women discovered the tomb empty, pondered its meaning, and reported to the remaining disciples. Only the Beloved Disciple, likely the "eyewitness" behind the Fourth Gospel, was one who believed upon finding the tomb empty. No other disciple did. But for most disciples, the empty tomb was not enough. Thus the risen Jesus appears.

We see similar movements of faith in our own lives. We find our own empty tombs, signifiers of something greater. But often we do not grasp the full meaning until later, until something equivalent to a resurrection appearance. Let us be attentive to the empty tomb signs and experiences in our lives that leave us pondering, wondering how God is acting in the world. It could be that we will experience a resurrection, new life from death, meaning from loss.

✦ Where do I see signs of the reality of resurrection?

Brief Silence

Prayer

Father of life, Author of love, in raising your Son from the grave, all of creation has been reborn. May the life and love manifested in the paschal mystery be a constant and lasting reality in our lives. We ask this through Christ, our risen Lord. **Amen.**

We use water to remind us of our baptisms. May God bless this water and bless all of us, so that, by his grace, we may be recreated in Easter peace . . .

Prayer

Lord Jesus, you appeared to Thomas the disciple who doubted, and gave him the beatitude you give to us. May we who have not seen still believe, so that through this belief we might have life in your name. **Amen.**

Gospel   John 20:19-31

On the evening of that first day of the week, when the doors were locked, where the disciples were, for fear of the Jews, Jesus came and stood in their midst and said to them, "Peace be with you." When he had said this, he showed them his hands and his side. The disciples rejoiced when they saw the Lord. Jesus said to them again, "Peace be with you. As the Father has sent me, so I send you." And when he had said this, he breathed on them and said to them, "Receive the Holy Spirit. Whose sins you forgive are forgiven them, and whose sins you retain are retained."

Thomas, called Didymus, one of the Twelve, was not with them when Jesus came. So the other disciples said to him, "We have seen the Lord." But he said to them, "Unless I see the mark of the nails in his hands and put my finger into the nailmarks and put my hand into his side, I will not believe."

Now a week later his disciples were again inside and Thomas was with them. Jesus came, although the doors were locked, and stood in their midst and said, "Peace be with you." Then he said to Thomas, "Put your finger here and see my hands, and bring your hand and put it into my side, and do not be unbelieving, but believe." Thomas answered and said to him, "My Lord and my God!"

Jesus said to him, "Have you come to believe because you have seen me? Blessed are those who have not seen and have believed."

Now, Jesus did many other signs in the presence of his disciples that are not written in this book. But these are written that you may come to believe that Jesus is the Christ, the Son of God, and that through this belief you may have life in his name.

Brief Silence

For Reflection

Though the disciples had been witness to the risen Lord on Easter Sunday evening, Thomas was absent, and so he functions as a disciple for all of us. In a sense, we stand in the person of Thomas. We were not present that Easter Sunday evening. And perhaps, like Thomas, we reply, "seeing is believing." The beatitude that Jesus speaks to Thomas is meant for each of us: "Blessed are those who have not seen and have believed."

The church gives us this reading on the Second Sunday of Easter, as that is when Thomas had his experience of the risen Lord. Though we are not given the opportunity to put our finger in the nail marks (and the gospel doesn't say that Thomas did that), we, like Thomas, may condition our belief on seeing.

The gift Jesus gives his disciples is "peace." It is not a peace that the world gives, that is, merely an absence of war. But the peace Jesus gives is a serenity in the face of life. The gift is a sense of calm knowing that Jesus is "my Lord and my God," and that there is nothing in this life that can separate him from me.

✦ Have I ever been swallowed up in Thomas-like skepticism and cynicism? How was that "doubt" transformed into hope and trust?

Brief Silence

Prayer

Hear the prayers of this community, O God, whom you gather at your table to remember in the "breaking of bread" your Son's passion, death, and resurrection. May his peace and spirit enable us to be your ministers of reconciliation and forgiveness in our homes and communities. **Amen.**

Water will be used to remind us of our baptisms. Let us ask God to send his Spirit upon this water and upon us, so that we may be faithful to the baptism we received . . .

Prayer

Lord Jesus, you appeared to your assembled disciples multiple times to demonstrate your resurrection from the dead. May that same spirit of resurrection inspire our own lives so that we may stir with Easter joy. **Amen.**

Gospel   **Luke 24:35-48**

The two disciples recounted what had taken place on the way, and how Jesus was made known to them in the breaking of bread.

While they were still speaking about this, he stood in their midst and said to them, "Peace be with you." But they were startled and terrified and thought that they were seeing a ghost. Then he said to them, "Why are you troubled? And why do questions arise in your hearts? Look at my hands and my feet, that it is I myself. Touch me and see, because a ghost does not have flesh and bones as you can see I have." And as he said this, he showed them his hands and his feet. While they were still incredulous for joy and were amazed, he asked them, "Have you anything here to eat?" They gave him a piece of baked fish; he took it and ate it in front of them.

He said to them, "These are my words that I spoke to you while I was still with you, that everything written about me in the law of Moses and in the prophets and psalms must be fulfilled." Then he opened their minds to understand the Scriptures. And he said to them, "Thus it is written that the Christ would suffer and rise from the dead on the third day and that repentance, for the forgiveness of sins, would be preached in his name to all the nations, beginning from Jerusalem. You are witnesses of these things."

Brief Silence

For Reflection

Now that we are in the third week of Easter, we hear yet another story of a resurrection appearance of Jesus. There are a number of different Easter stories that appeal to us on a variety of levels. Initially, the story was the finding of the empty tomb. Then, we had a story of the appearance of Jesus to the disciples without Thomas, followed by one with Thomas. Thomas says he will not believe unless he probes the nail marks. Now we have another story where the risen Jesus eats a meal. He is said to have flesh and bones. He is not a ghost. His eating baked fish virtually confirms that.

If we didn't understand with the empty tomb, if we didn't understand when Jesus appeared to even Thomas, now there is another appearance where he graphically demonstrates that he is present amongst them. Of course, each of the three stories we are referring to are from different gospel writers: the empty tomb (Mark), the appearance to Thomas (John), and now the risen Jesus eating fish (Luke). The church gives us these texts on successive Sundays to confirm for us that Jesus truly rose from the dead.

✦ When was the last time I confronted my own "ignorance" about something or someone?

Brief Silence

Prayer

Father of life, hear our Easter prayers. In our work to make these prayers a reality, may your love be perfected in us—love revealed in the resurrection of your Christ, in whose name we offer these prayers. **Amen.**

We will use this water to remind us of our baptisms into the life of the risen Christ. Let us ask God to bless this water and bless all of us, so that, by his grace, we may be recreated in Easter peace . . .

Prayer

Lord Jesus, you are the Good Shepherd who lays down his life for his sheep. Keep us gathered around you, attentive to your voice. And should we be scattered, give us attentive ears so that we may hear you and return to the fold. **Amen.**

Gospel   **John 10:11-18**

Jesus said: "I am the good shepherd. A good shepherd lays down his life for the sheep. A hired man, who is not a shepherd and whose sheep are not his own, sees a wolf coming and leaves the sheep and runs away, and the wolf catches and scatters them. This is because he works for pay and has no concern for the sheep. I am the good shepherd, and I know mine and mine know me, just as the Father knows me and I know the Father; and I will lay down my life for the sheep. I have other sheep that do not belong to this fold. These also I must lead, and they will hear my voice, and there will be one flock, one shepherd. This is why the Father loves me, because I lay down my life in order to take it up again. No one takes it from me, but I lay it down on my own. I have power to lay it down, and power to take it up again. This command I have received from my Father."

Brief Silence

For Reflection

Today we celebrate "Good Shepherd" Sunday as we read this famous gospel story from John. We are no longer in the realm of resurrection appearance stories, but now we have entered the world of Jesus' "I AM" parabolic discourse. The image of a shepherd is certainly one rooted in antiquity. There are not as many shepherds today as there were then. Yet, even though most of us probably do not know any shepherds, or have even seen any recently, we are all familiar with the image.

Jesus makes a distinction in this discourse about himself as the "good shepherd" and a "hired man" who works for money. The latter has no real concern for the sheep. He is in it only for the pay. Jesus, on the other hand, loves the sheep; he lays down his life for them. The hired hand will run away at the first sign of danger, and the sheep will be scattered. As we consider this in our own time we can see the many Christians, many of us, who have been scattered. As we listen for the voice of the Good Shepherd and come to him, we will be reunited.

✦ Where do I hear the voice of the Good Shepherd today?

Brief Silence

Prayer

Hear, O God, the prayers of your children gathered at your table. Open our hearts and spirits to hear the voice of your Son leading us to the fulfillment of your kingdom. We make these prayers in the name of your Son, Jesus the Good Shepherd. **Amen.**

In the waters of baptism we were recreated in the life of the Easter Christ. We begin our Eucharist by using water to remember our baptisms, asking that the Spirit that came upon us may continue to fill us with God's grace and Christ's peace . . .

Prayer

Father, you are the vine grower and we are the branches. Keep us attached to the vine, your Son Jesus. Prune us so that we may produce more fruit, for our life and well-being come from the vine. **Amen.**

Gospel   John 15:1-8

Jesus said to his disciples: "I am the true vine, and my Father is the vine grower. He takes away every branch in me that does not bear fruit, and every one that does he prunes so that it bears more fruit. You are already pruned because of the word that I spoke to you. Remain in me, as I remain in you. Just as a branch cannot bear fruit on its own unless it remains on the vine, so neither can you unless you remain in me. I am the vine, you are the branches. Whoever remains in me and I in him will bear much fruit, because without me you can do nothing. Anyone who does not remain in me will be thrown out like a branch and wither; people will gather them and throw them into a fire and they will be burned. If you remain in me and my words remain in you, ask for whatever you want and it will be done for you. By this is my Father glorified, that you bear much fruit and become my disciples."

Brief Silence

For Reflection

The image used in today's gospel is polyvalent. It can be under-stood in a number of ways. For one, Jesus says that the branches that do bear fruit are pruned to bear more. We might wonder why these fruit-bearing branches need to be pruned at all?! Isn't it enough to cut off the branches that do not bear fruit? No, for the vine grower, merely producing fruit is not enough. He knows that the branch can produce more. And anyone with gardening experi-ence would agree.

And thus Jesus reminds us of the vine grower's role. Not only does the vine grower ensure the vine's viability, but he prunes branches to produce fruit, and cuts away those that do not pro-duce any fruit. In a stark vision of the end time, Jesus takes yet another step to say that those branches that have been cut away will be thrown into the fire to be burned. Such apocalyptic images are rare in this gospel, but present nonetheless.

Where are we in the metaphor? We are the branches, fully aware that no branch can produce fruit on its own. We must re-main attached to the vine to bear fruit. So as not to be lopped off, we remain in Jesus.

✦ How does our connectedness to Christ make our parish more than just another charitable or humanitarian organization?

Brief Silence

Prayer

Hear our Easter prayers, O Lord. May your words forever be a part of us; may your peace forever reign over us; may your love forever unite us as your children. We ask these things in the name of your Son, the risen One. **Amen.**

We will use this water to remind us of our baptisms. May God send his Spirit upon it and upon us, so that the Word of God may continue to recreate us in God's love . . .

Prayer

Jesus, you are the incarnation of God's love in the world. As your disciples, give us the freedom to love without counting the cost, to do more rather than less, to be your presence in our day. **Amen.**

Gospel   John 15:9-17

Jesus said to his disciples: "As the Father loves me, so I also love you. Remain in my love. If you keep my commandments, you will remain in my love, just as I have kept my Father's commandments and remain in his love.

"I have told you this so that my joy may be in you and your joy might be complete. This is my commandment: love one another as I love you. No one has greater love than this, to lay down one's life for one's friends. You are my friends if you do what I command you. I no longer call you slaves, because a slave does not know what his master is doing. I have called you friends, because I have told you everything I have heard from my Father. It was not you who chose me, but I who chose you and appointed you to go and bear fruit that will remain, so that whatever you ask the Father in my name he may give you. This I command you: love one another."

Brief Silence

For Reflection

When we are young we learn a list of "dos" and "don'ts." The list is seemingly endless. Even the Old Testament had a list, which today we refer to as the Ten Commandments. But Jesus gives us a command in today's gospel that supersedes all others. It is simply this: "love one another." Of course, with a command like this, it can be seductive to return to a checklist! How much easier would it be to maintain a checklist, such as, going to church, celebrating the sacraments, fasting on Ash Wednesday and Good Friday. But the command issued by Jesus is much more difficult. A command to love knows no bounds, knows no checklist. By this command Jesus invites us to an adult spirituality, no longer satisfied by keeping a list. Love does not count the cost or put a limit on what price is too high. Love can always do more. Love is based on a personal relationship with another that is not transactional but self-giving. As Jesus says in the gospel, his love for his friends reaches the point of laying down his own life for them. We receive from Jesus a command simple but demanding: "love one another."

✦ What does it mean to be a "friend" of God, as opposed to simply believing in the existence of God?

Brief Silence

Prayer

O God of unfathomable love, hear our Easter prayers. Make us worthy to be your "friends," in our compassion and support for our friends here, in our seeking what is right and acceptable in your eyes, in our faithfulness to your commandment to love one another as you love us. We ask these things through Christ Jesus, our brother and friend. **Amen.**

In baptism we have been called to be witnesses of Christ Jesus. Let us ask God to send his Spirit upon this water that we will use to remember our baptisms—and may that same Spirit again descend upon us, sending us forth to realize the hope of our call . . .

Prayer

Lord Jesus, you reign with God in heaven, having ascended there after your resurrection. Give us the assurance that heaven is our destiny as well, when we will be united with you, and reunited with all of our loved ones. **Amen.**

Gospel   Mark 16:15-20

Jesus said to his disciples: "Go into the whole world and proclaim the gospel to every creature. Whoever believes and is baptized will be saved; whoever does not believe will be condemned. These signs will accompany those who believe: in my name they will drive out demons, they will speak new languages. They will pick up serpents with their hands, and if they drink any deadly thing, it will not harm them. They will lay hands on the sick, and they will recover."

So then the Lord Jesus, after he spoke to them, was taken up into heaven and took his seat at the right hand of God. But they went forth and preached everywhere, while the Lord worked with them and confirmed the word through accompanying signs.

Brief Silence

For Reflection

The notes in the New American Bible make clear that Mark's gospel ended at 16:8. But it seems that some copyists did not like the ending to be one where all the disciples run away because they were afraid! And so we have a multiplicity of endings attested to by different manuscripts. What we refer to as Mark 16:9-20 is one such ending, and it is certainly considered canonical, inspired, and authoritative, but it was not part of the "original" gospel. It was written by a later author.

Among other things, Mark 16:9-20 answers the question of the Gentile mission, or why there are so many Gentiles in a movement that was initially Jewish. The answer is that Jesus gave them the command, "Go into the whole world / and proclaim the gospel to every creature." In a sense, this is Mark's version of Matthew's more elegant Great Commandment (Matt 28:19-20). The Markan gospel passage, and the gospel itself, concludes with an echo of 1 Timothy 3:16 and Luke 24:15, namely that Jesus was "taken up" into heaven. This episode answers the question, where is Jesus now? He is in heaven, seated at the right hand of God.

✦ Most of us are neither teachers nor preachers. So how do I fulfill Jesus' commission to be his "witness" in my own Jerusalem?

Brief Silence

Prayer

Father, in raising the Lord Jesus from the grave into heaven, you have given hope to us and to all humanity. Hear the prayers we make to you in the name of Jesus your Christ, the source and life of that hope, who lives and reigns with you forever and ever. **Amen.**

This water will be used to remind us of our baptisms. May the Spirit of God come down upon this water and upon all of us, consecrating us in God's truth and grace . . .

Prayer

Jesus our Advocate, you prayed for us that our joy may be complete. As your followers we long to be with you. May your advocacy on our behalf strengthen us during our journey in this world, so that we may celebrate life eternal with you. **Amen.**

Gospel   John 17:11b-19

Lifting up his eyes to heaven, Jesus prayed, saying: "Holy Father, keep them in your name that you have given me, so that they may be one just as we are one. When I was with them I protected them in your name that you gave me, and I guarded them, and none of them was lost except the son of destruction, in order that the Scripture might be fulfilled. But now I am coming to you. I speak this in the world so that they may share my joy completely. I gave them your word, and the world hated them, because they do not belong to the world any more than I belong to the world. I do not ask that you take them out of the world but that you keep them from the evil one. They do not belong to the world any more than I belong to the world. Consecrate them in the truth. Your word is truth. As you sent me into the world, so I sent them into the world. And I consecrate myself for them, so that they also may be consecrated in truth."

Brief Silence

For Reflection

In today's gospel Jesus prays a final prayer to the Father prior to
his own arrest and ultimate crucifixion. What must have been
going through his mind at that time? He was definitely concerned
for his friends, those whom the Father had given and entrusted
to Jesus. He prays for them, not that they may be taken out of the
world, but that they may be kept from evil, safe from harm, while
living in it. Jesus protected his friends while he was with them, but
he will be with them no longer.

Jesus' desire for his friends, and that includes us, is that they
may share his joy completely. He knows that the world is a tough,
sometimes violent place. He will lose his life in a contest with vio-
lence. And yet, he does not take us out of the world. He gives us
the ability to live in it, while asking the Father to keep us from the
evil one. This final prayer and petition tells us a great deal about
Jesus, his relationship with the Father, and his relationship with
us. How fortunate we are to have him as our advocate.

✦ In what ways does my life reflect the fact that I share the joy
of Jesus completely?

Brief Silence

Prayer

Gracious God, hear the prayers of the people your Son has gathered before you. Consecrate us in your Word so that we may speak
your truth in justice and mirror your never-failing love in works
of reconciliation. We offer these prayers to you in the name of
your Son, the risen Jesus. **Amen.**

Gathered in this place, we have come to celebrate God's Spirit dwelling among us. Let us give voice to that Spirit in the prayers we now offer . . .

Prayer

Lord Jesus, you gave us the command and the ability to forgive sins. Stir up in our consciences opportunities to exercise this ministry in our daily lives, so that we may extend your mercy in our own time and place. **Amen.**

Gospel   **John 15:26-27; 16:12-15 (or John 20:19-23)**

Jesus said to his disciples: "When the Advocate comes whom I will send you from the Father, the Spirit of truth that proceeds from the Father, he will testify to me. And you also testify, because you have been with me from the beginning.

"I have much more to tell you, but you cannot bear it now. But when he comes, the Spirit of truth, he will guide you to all truth. He will not speak on his own, but he will speak what he hears, and will declare to you the things that are coming. He will glorify me, because he will take from what is mine and declare it to you. Everything that the Father has is mine; for this reason I told you that he will take from what is mine and declare it to you."

Brief Silence

For Reflection

When Christians think of Pentecost, we often have the image of the disciples in the Upper Room, with the tongues of fire descending upon each before they preach to Jerusalem. But that is Luke's story in the Acts of the Apostles; today we have John's version of the handing on of the Spirit. Interestingly, this event happens not on Pentecost, as Luke would have it, but on Easter Sunday evening! This is the same evening on which the risen Jesus appeared to the assembled disciples without Thomas. So we get our liturgical timetable from Luke, but our theology today comes from the Gospel of John.

Jesus comes to be with the disciples and to give them the gift of peace and also the gift of the Holy Spirit. The disciples receive the Spirit and the ability to forgive sins. By his death and resurrection Jesus has conquered the cosmic power of sin. Now it is the disciples' role, and our own, to continue this mission by forgiving individual sins for the same Spirit has been given to us. Forgiveness is not limited to sacramental confession. As Christians, we are to forgive. It is a hallmark of our identity, given to us by Jesus himself.

✦ Are there persons whom I need to forgive?

Brief Silence

Prayer

Father of life, hear our prayers. Recreate us in your Holy Spirit so that we may be a source of forgiveness and a community of hope for our hurting world. We make these prayers in the name of Jesus, the risen Christ. **Amen.**

To God, our Father and Redeemer, let us ask his forgiveness for our sins and failings . . .

Prayer

Lord God Almighty, you revealed yourself as a trinity. As disciples, we were baptized into your life. May our baptism give us the motivation to teach and baptize in your triune name, for you are one God, forever and ever. **Amen.**

Gospel   Matt 28:16-20

The eleven disciples went to Galilee, to the mountain to which Jesus had ordered them. When they all saw him, they worshiped, but they doubted. Then Jesus approached and said to them, "All power in heaven and on earth has been given to me. Go, therefore, and make disciples of all nations, baptizing them in the name of the Father, and of the Son, and of the Holy Spirit, teaching them to observe all that I have commanded you. And behold, I am with you always, until the end of the age."

Brief Silence

For Reflection

Though *trinitas* is a Latin word and therefore not found in the New Testament, which was written in Greek, there are many "triadic" texts that speak of Father/God, Son, Spirit. Passages like the one for today would be considered "triadic," and they would give rise to full-blown trinitarian theology in later centuries.

The gospel scene is after Easter, but in Galilee. According to Matthew, this is the first and only appearance of the risen Jesus to his disciples. Still, the disciples doubt. They receive the command that has been referred to as "the Great Commandment": "Go, therefore, and make disciples of all nations, / baptizing them in the name of the Father, / and of the Son, and of the Holy Spirit." Matthew's baptismal formula for making a disciple is the same as what Christians use today. Based on this "Great Commandment," Christianity has become a worldwide religion. From a mountaintop in Galilee, those initial disciples made other disciples by baptism, who made still more disciples by baptism, and so on, until our very day. Discipleship is founded on baptism into the life of the Trinity.

✦ What difference does it make that I profess a triune God?

Brief Silence

Prayer

Hear the prayers we offer to you, O God of compassion and mercy, O God who redeems us and restores us to life, O God who lives in us and through us. We offer these prayers, O Father, in your Spirit of love, in the name of your Son, Christ Jesus. **Amen.**

To prepare ourselves to offer this sacrament of the Body and Blood of the Lord, let us begin by calling to mind our sins, asking the constant mercy of God, who invites us to this table . . .

Prayer

Lord Jesus Christ, you give us your very self in the eucharistic bread and wine to sustain us on our way. Upon receiving the Eucharist, may we become sustenance for others by our own words and deeds, furthering your mission on earth. **Amen.**

Gospel   **Mark 14:12-16, 22-26**

On the first day of the Feast of Unleavened Bread, when they sacrificed the Passover lamb, Jesus' disciples said to him, "Where do you want us to go and prepare for you to eat the Passover?" He sent two of his disciples and said to them, "Go into the city and a man will meet you, carrying a jar of water. Follow him. Wherever he enters, say to the master of the house, 'The Teacher says, "Where is my guest room where I may eat the Passover with my disciples?"' Then he will show you a large upper room furnished and ready. Make the preparations for us there." The disciples then went off, entered the city, and found it just as he had told them; and they prepared the Passover.

While they were eating, he took bread, said the blessing, broke it, gave it to them, and said, "Take it; this is my body." Then he took a cup, gave thanks, and gave it to them, and they all drank from it. He said to them, "This is my blood of the covenant, which will be shed for many. Amen, I say to you, I shall not drink again the fruit of the vine until the day when I drink it new in the kingdom of God." Then, after singing a hymn, they went out to the Mount of Olives.

Brief Silence

For Reflection

The graphic image of "body and blood" comes from the ancient world where the body is flesh and "blood is life" (Deut 12:23). The bread and wine of the eucharistic banquet become the Body and Blood of Christ, in a *transubstantive* way.

The gospel reading is Mark's version of the Last Supper, which for him was in the context of the Passover meal. Even the singing of the hymn, which Mark is certain to include, is an integral part of the Passover to this very day. But according to the Synoptic Gospels (Matthew, Mark, and Luke) Jesus gave new meaning to the Passover meal. The bread that he takes, blesses, breaks, and shares is his Body. The cup of thanksgiving that is shared is his covenantal Blood. Anyone who has been to a Jewish Seder meal likely has a profound appreciation for these symbols of bread and wine, and how they were appropriated in the Christian tradition. The Passover meal, which commemorated the people's delivery from Egypt, would now commemorate Jesus' death and ultimate delivery from death to resurrection. Our participation in consuming the bread and wine is a participation in the life, death, and subsequent resurrection of Jesus.

✦ How do my own family rituals at dinnertime and around the family table reflect the Eucharist?

Brief Silence

Prayer

Hear our prayers, O God. May the bread and wine of the Eucharist transform us into the bread of generosity and the wine of joy for our hurting world. We ask these things in the name of Jesus, the Bread of Life. **Amen.**

Let us begin our celebration of these sacred mysteries by asking the healing forgiveness of God for our sins and failings . . .

Prayer

Lord Jesus Christ, you came into this world but the world did not understand you. Give us the courage to stay true to you even when we are misunderstood for doing so. May our faithfulness to you and your message be a source of consolation and peace. **Amen.**

Gospel   Mark 3:20-35

Jesus came home with his disciples. Again the crowd gathered, making it impossible for them even to eat. When his relatives heard of this they set out to seize him, for they said, "He is out of his mind." The scribes who had come from Jerusalem said, "He is possessed by Beelzebul," and "By the prince of demons he drives out demons."

Summoning them, he began to speak to them in parables, "How can Satan drive out Satan? If a kingdom is divided against itself, that kingdom cannot stand. And if a house is divided against itself, that house will not be able to stand. And if Satan has risen up against himself and is divided, he cannot stand; that is the end of him. But no one can enter a strong man's house to plunder his property unless he first ties up the strong man. Then he can plunder the house. Amen, I say to you, all sins and all blasphemies that people utter will be forgiven them. But whoever blasphemes against the Holy Spirit will never have forgiveness, but is guilty of an everlasting sin." For they had said, "He has an unclean spirit."

His mother and his brothers arrived. Standing outside they sent word to him and called him. A crowd seated around him told him, "Your mother and your brothers and your sisters are outside asking for you." But he said to them in reply, "Who are my mother and my brothers?" And looking around at those seated in the circle he said, "Here are my mother and my brothers. For whoever does the will of God is my brother and sister and mother."

Brief Silence

For Reflection

Today we have a story about Jesus' family. In between this story there is another about scribes from Jerusalem attributing Jesus' power to Beelzebul, a name for the devil. The gospel begins with a snippet that is unique to Mark: Jesus' relatives come to get him, saying, "He is out of his mind." This is hardly the image we have of Jesus' own family. But, we are reminded that in Mark, the first canonical gospel that was written, there is no infancy narrative, no annunciation to Mary or Joseph's dream that he should take Mary as his wife.

Wrapped in this story about Jesus' family is another about scribes from Jerusalem who attribute his power to the devil. Not surprisingly, Jesus disputes that. The stakes are high. Jesus seems to be getting it from all sides. His family, who raised him, and the scribes, who are experts in the law, do not understand him. He is thought to be out of his mind by some and by others to be possessed by a demon. Neither is very flattering! But Jesus stays true to who he is and counters each assault. The community he is forming is something new, based not on familial relations, but stronger than family.

✦ What is my reaction when I seem to be getting it from all sides?

Brief Silence

Prayer

O Lord, may the prayers we offer with one voice make us one in heart and spirit, as well. Grant these prayers that we make to you in the name of Christ Jesus, the Lord. **Amen.**

To prepare ourselves to celebrate these sacred mysteries, let us place our hearts before God, seeking his mercy for our sins and failings . . .

Prayer

Jesus, you are the Master Teacher and we are the learners. Grant us the wisdom to discern the meaning of your parables, so that we might be your followers and thus lead others to you. **Amen.**

Gospel   Mark 4:26-34

Jesus said to the crowds: "This is how it is with the kingdom of God; it is as if a man were to scatter seed on the land and would sleep and rise night and day and through it all the seed would sprout and grow, he knows not how. Of its own accord the land yields fruit, first the blade, then the ear, then the full grain in the ear. And when the grain is ripe, he wields the sickle at once, for the harvest has come."

He said, "To what shall we compare the kingdom of God, or what parable can we use for it? It is like a mustard seed that, when it is sown in the ground, is the smallest of all the seeds on the earth. But once it is sown, it springs up and becomes the largest of plants and puts forth large branches, so that the birds of the sky can dwell in its shade." With many such parables he spoke the word to them as they were able to understand it. Without parables he did not speak to them, but to his own disciples he explained everything in private.

Brief Silence

For Reflection

We are familiar with the gospel image of seed being scattered, such as the parable of the sower and seed, wherein the seed represents God's word. That parable is found in Mark 4:1-20 with parallels in Matthew and Luke. But today's gospel tells a different story. God's kingdom is likened to a man scattering seed upon the ground, and the seed grows without the man knowing how. Perhaps the meaning of this parable was meant to be self-evident, for it is not explained.

We are told that Jesus spoke to the crowds in parables, but he explained them to his disciples privately. We might wonder why Jesus would not explain the parables to the crowds. Our somewhat disturbing answer comes in the same chapter, where Jesus tells his disciples, "The mystery of the kingdom of God has been granted to you. But to those outside everything comes in parables, so that / 'they may look and see but not perceive, / and hear and listen but not understand, / in order that they may not be converted and be forgiven'" (Mark 4:11-12). It may sound strange to us that Jesus would not want those on the outside to be converted and forgiven. But like other Markan passages, this tells us a great deal about the community for whom Mark wrote, and its sense of being persecuted. The disciples whom Jesus called formed bonds stronger than family. They were chosen to live in relationship with him and one another. Though he taught in enigmatic parables, he explained all to his disciples. Those on the outside understood the words, but not the hidden meaning of the parables.

✦ What do gardening and the planting and nurturing of seeds teach me about everyday life?

Brief Silence

Prayer

Accept these prayers, O God, and, with the faith of the mustard seed, may our smallest acts of kindness and justice bring your kingdom to reality in our own time and place. In Jesus' name, we pray. **Amen.**

Today, six months before we celebrate the birth of Jesus, we remember John the Baptist, the last of the prophets, who heralded the coming of the Messiah into our broken world. As we prepare to celebrate the Eucharist, let us call to mind our failure to recognize Christ's presence in our midst and ask the forgiveness of our loving Father . . .

Prayer

Lord Jesus, your coming was heralded by John the Baptist. May we who are attentive to you heed also the call of your prophets and forerunners, like John. May we hear their message in our own time and place. **Amen.**

Gospel   Luke 1:57-66, 80

When the time arrived for Elizabeth to have her child she gave birth to a son. Her neighbors and relatives heard that the Lord had shown his great mercy toward her, and they rejoiced with her. When they came on the eighth day to circumcise the child, they were going to call him Zechariah after his father, but his mother said in reply, "No. He will be called John." But they answered her, "There is no one among your relatives who has this name." So they made signs, asking his father what he wished him to be called. He asked for a tablet and wrote, "John is his name," and all were amazed. Immediately his mouth was opened, his tongue freed, and he spoke blessing God. Then fear came upon all their neighbors, and all these matters were discussed throughout the hill country of Judea. All who heard these things took them to heart, saying, "What, then, will this child be?" For surely the hand of the Lord was with him.

The child grew and became strong in spirit, and he was in the desert until the day of his manifestation to Israel.

Brief Silence

For Reflection

Luke is the sole voice in the New Testament telling us about the familial relationship between Elizabeth and Mary, making Jesus and John the Baptist cousins. Perhaps surprisingly, we don't hear much about either Zechariah or Joseph. Luke tells us more about the women, and this might be a nod to the influence mothers have in our lives, and therefore in the lives of Jesus and John.

As Luke tells the story, Elizabeth was three months pregnant when Mary received the news that she would bear a son. Liturgically speaking, this feast is thus three months later than the annunciation (March 25) or six months prior to Christmas. The newborn John is a herald of the Messiah, even by his very birth. Like the marvelous conception and birth of Jesus, John too has something marvelous surrounding his conception and birth. Like the forebears in faith, Zechariah and Elizabeth are too old to have children. But God has other plans.

We are reminded that family is the domestic church. It is there that children first learn the faith. And actions certainly speak more loudly than words. May our families, like those of Mary and Elizabeth, be places of safety, nourishment, love, care, and faith.

✦ What does my family "teach" by its actions?

Brief Silence

Prayer

Hear our prayers, O gracious God. Inspired by the prophetic ministry of John the Baptist, may we prepare our homes and hearts to welcome into our world the dawning of your Light, Christ Jesus, in whose name we make these prayers. **Amen.**

As we gather to celebrate these sacred mysteries, let us begin by seeking God's forgiveness and mercy . . .

Prayer

Lord God, you sent Jesus your Son into the world to heal the sick and raise the dead. May we be worthy of the name disciple by our actions to heal those who hurt and raise those who have been brought low. **Amen.**

Gospel   Mark 5:21-24, 35b-43 (or Mark 5:21-43)

When Jesus had crossed again in the boat to the other side, a large crowd gathered around him, and he stayed close to the sea. One of the synagogue officials, named Jairus, came forward. Seeing him he fell at his feet and pleaded earnestly with him, saying, "My daughter is at the point of death. Please, come lay your hands on her that she may get well and live." He went off with him, and a large crowd followed him and pressed upon him.

While he was still speaking, people from the synagogue official's house arrived and said, "Your daughter has died; why trouble the teacher any longer?" Disregarding the message that was reported, Jesus said to the synagogue official, "Do not be afraid; just have faith." He did not allow anyone to accompany him inside except Peter, James, and John, the brother of James. When they arrived at the house of the synagogue official, he caught sight of a commotion, people weeping and wailing loudly. So he went in and said to them, "Why this commotion and weeping? The child is not dead but asleep." And they ridiculed him. Then he put them all out. He took along the child's father and mother and those who were with him and entered the room where the child was. He took the child by the hand and said to her, *"Talitha koum,"* which means, "Little girl, I say to you, arise!" The girl, a child of twelve, arose immediately and walked around. At that they were utterly astounded. He gave strict orders that no one should know this and said that she should be given something to eat.

Brief Silence

For Reflection

The story of the woman touching Jesus' garment is sandwiched between the story of Jairus's daughter being raised from the dead. Mark tells the stories with attention to certain details. For example, when the woman with a hemorrhage reaches out to touch only Jesus' garments, power immediately flows out of him. He is unaware of who touched him. When he finds out, he tells the woman that her faith has made her well.

The story that forms a bookend around the woman with a hemorrhage is the raising of Jairus's daughter. Here Jesus continues his confrontation with evil, this time death. And he is victorious. Before he even arrives at the home, the twelve-year-old girl is pronounced dead. Jesus raises the girl and admonishes the three disciples who were with him not to say anything.

Jesus' power is on clear display. Merely touching his garment with an act of faith is enough to heal somebody. Jesus himself raises the dead to new life. His identity is coming into sharper focus as we journey with him through this gospel.

✦ Have I known a parent whose love for his or her child reflected the love of God in a unique way?

Brief Silence

Prayer

O God, you know our needs before we realize them ourselves. Hear these prayers we offer to you for all your people, that you will bless all our brothers and sisters with your healing peace and reconciling love. We ask this in the name of Jesus, the healer and teacher. **Amen.**

Let us begin our celebration of the Eucharist by humbly placing our hearts before God, confident of his forgiveness for our sins and failings . . .

Prayer

Lord Jesus, you were the object of prejudice and narrow-minded thinking by those who should have known you best. When we face opposition because of our belief in you, give us your understanding and consolation. **Amen.**

Gospel   **Mark 6:1-6a**

Jesus departed from there and came to his native place, accompanied by his disciples. When the sabbath came he began to teach in the synagogue, and many who heard him were astonished. They said, "Where did this man get all this? What kind of wisdom has been given him? What mighty deeds are wrought by his hands! Is he not the carpenter, the son of Mary, and the brother of James and Joses and Judas and Simon? And are not his sisters here with us?" And they took offense at him. Jesus said to them, "A prophet is not without honor except in his native place and among his own kin and in his own house." So he was not able to perform any mighty deed there, apart from curing a few sick people by laying his hands on them. He was amazed at their lack of faith.

Brief Silence

For Reflection

The townspeople knew Jesus from the time he was a little boy, but he had grown up and become his own person. Those from his hometown had pegged him, put him in a box. He was the "carpenter," the son of Mary. They knew him and knew his family. Who was he to teach them?

In response, Jesus refers to himself as a prophet without honor in his own country, town, and even in his own house. We are reminded of the adage, "familiarity breeds contempt." Those who were closest to Jesus for most of his life did not see him for who he was but for who they determined him to be.

As a result, he could do no mighty work there except a few minor healings! In this early gospel we hear something of the resistance Jesus faced and the resulting limitation in his ability to perform mighty works. Jesus was amazed at their unbelief. Their own limited understanding and their inability to perceive who he was limited the works he was able to perform.

✦ Have I ever known someone who possessed the courageous, unwavering faith of a "prophet"?

Brief Silence

Prayer

We come to you in hope, O Lord, knowing that you will hear the prayers we ask in faith. May your Spirit of wisdom and truth rest upon us always, so that we may be prophets of your great love. In Jesus' name, we pray. **Amen.**

Let us begin our celebration of these sacred mysteries by calling to mind our sins . . .

Prayer

God Almighty, you sent your Son to call his disciples, and from them he sent forth twelve. Send us too so that we might evangelize your Son to all those we meet and share with them the good news of salvation. **Amen.**

Gospel   Mark 6:7-13

Jesus summoned the Twelve and began to send them out two by two and gave them authority over unclean spirits. He instructed them to take nothing for the journey but a walking stick—no food, no sack, no money in their belts. They were, however, to wear sandals but not a second tunic. He said to them, "Wherever you enter a house, stay there until you leave. Whatever place does not welcome you or listen to you, leave there and shake the dust off your feet in testimony against them." So they went off and preached repentance. The Twelve drove out many demons, and they anointed with oil many who were sick and cured them.

Brief Silence

For Reflection

Even though the disciples will never achieve the rank of master, in the Gospel of Mark today Jesus gives the Twelve authority. He sends them on mission in six groups of two. This will be the model for Christian evangelization. Their preaching is basically that of John the Baptist and the early days of Jesus himself, "Repent." The disciples also exercised their authority over evil, over the demons, over sickness, and over the unclean spirits. The authority that Jesus shared with his disciples for this mission meant that they too, like him, were agents of inclusion. They brought those from the margins into a relationship of wholeness. Like him, their deeds were coupled with preaching. The demand for repentance was paramount; and we can surmise that the demand was not received well by all, as Jesus' instructions for "shak[ing] the dust off your feet" indicate. Not all disciples were chosen for this mission, but only the Twelve. The mission is to go out preaching and performing works of mercy. This probably doesn't sound much like parish plans today for the "new evangelization." But this is the "mission of the Twelve" and we might find something worthy of emulation here.

✦ When have I experienced true repentance—when have I found the grace and courage to change course in my life?

Brief Silence

Prayer

O God, you reveal your limitless love to us in the compassion and forgiveness we give and receive. Hear these prayers and instill in us your grace so that we may be the means for realizing these prayers. In Jesus' name, we pray. **Amen.**

With humility and hope, let us ask God's forgiveness and peace for our sins and failings . . .

Prayer

Lord Jesus, your ministry among the crowds seemed all consuming and never ending. And still you looked on them with pity. When we have given all we can, refresh us with the spirit of self-service, so that we may extend your ministry in our own time and place. **Amen.**

Gospel   **Mark 6:30-34**

The apostles gathered together with Jesus and reported all they had done and taught. He said to them, "Come away by yourselves to a deserted place and rest a while." People were coming and going in great numbers, and they had no opportunity even to eat. So they went off in the boat by themselves to a deserted place. People saw them leaving and many came to know about it. They hastened there on foot from all the towns and arrived at the place before them.

When he disembarked and saw the vast crowd, his heart was moved with pity for them, for they were like sheep without a shepherd; and he began to teach them many things.

Brief Silence

For Reflection

By this time in the gospel narrative Jesus has attracted such attention he can get no "down time." Even when he and his disciples try to get away, the crowd flocks to them, like the ancient paparazzi! Jesus meets them, has compassion on them, and teaches them. All of this is a prelude to the multiplication of the loaves in Mark's Gospel 6:35-44), but next week we will hear John's version instead.

But in Mark's gospel, by the end of the day, the disciples display an attitude familiar to us: These people will want something to eat. Is that our problem? Let's get this crowd on the road so they can fend for themselves. The disciples seem indignant at Jesus' command to feed the crowd.

Significantly, Jesus sees that the crowd was "like sheep without a shepherd"—this line is used frequently in the Old Testament (Num 27:17; 1 Kgs 22:17; 2 Chr 18:16; Isa 13:14). The image invokes pastoral imagery rooted in Sacred Scripture. Jesus takes the role of shepherd of this flock, giving them sustenance by his teaching and the multiplication of loaves and fishes.

✦ Who are the "shepherds" in our culture?

Brief Silence

Prayer

Hear these prayers we offer, O God, and gather us together in your peace to be about the work of reconciliation and mercy. We ask these things in the name of your Son, Jesus Christ, our Shepherd and peace. **Amen.**

As we gather at the Lord's table to celebrate this Eucharist, let us begin by acknowledging our sins and failings, assured of God's reconciling love . . .

Prayer

Lord Jesus, you satisfy the hungry with the bread of everlasting life. Give that same bread to those who call on you, so that we may be satisfied with your presence. **Amen.**

Gospel   **John 6:1-15**

Jesus went across the Sea of Galilee. A large crowd followed him, because they saw the signs he was performing on the sick. Jesus went up on the mountain, and there he sat down with his disciples. The Jewish feast of Passover was near. When Jesus raised his eyes and saw that a large crowd was coming to him, he said to Philip, "Where can we buy enough food for them to eat?" He said this to test him, because he himself knew what he was going to do. Philip answered him, "Two hundred days' wages worth of food would not be enough for each of them to have a little." One of his disciples, Andrew, the brother of Simon Peter, said to him, "There is a boy here who has five barley loaves and two fish; but what good are these for so many?" Jesus said, "Have the people recline." Now there was a great deal of grass in that place. So the men reclined, about five thousand in number. Then Jesus took the loaves, gave thanks, and distributed them to those who were reclining, and also as much of the fish as they wanted. When they had had their fill, he said to his disciples, "Gather the fragments left over, so that nothing will be wasted." So they collected them, and filled twelve wicker baskets with fragments from the five barley loaves that had been more than they could eat. When the people saw the sign he had done, they said, "This is truly the Prophet, the one who is to come into the world." Since Jesus knew that they were going to come and carry him off to make him king, he withdrew again to the mountain alone.

Brief Silence

For Reflection

Last week we heard Mark's setup to the feeding of the five thousand, but this week we hear John's version rather than Mark's. The two stories have many similarities: two hundred denarii, five loaves and two fish, the crowd numbering five thousand men, and twelve baskets of leftovers, to name a few. But there are some differences to the stories as well.

John's theology is ultimately Christology. John has an intense focus on Jesus, who takes the initiative in asking Philip about feeding the people. And there is something equivalent to an editorial note saying that Jesus asked this question only to test him. Eucharistic overtones are also present here. Also, upon witnessing this sign (the multiplication of the loaves) the crowd explicitly recognizes Jesus as a prophet. No doubt the story of the prophet Elisha and the multiplication of the loaves from 2 Kings 4:42-44 was in mind. Jesus realized the crowd wanted to make him a king, so he makes a speedy solo exit.

The multiplication of the loaves, with its eucharistic overtones, its prominence on Jesus and his fulfilling human needs, and the growing recognition by the crowds that he must be a prophet demonstrate how pivotal this episode was and continues to be.

✦ How can my community take this Eucharist beyond the walls of the church?

Brief Silence

Prayer

One in spirit through the bond of peace, we join our hearts and voices in these prayers, O God. Grant them a favorable hearing and, by your grace, may we work together to make them a reality. In Jesus' name, we pray. **Amen.**

Trusting in the mercy of God, let us begin our celebration of the Eucharist by acknowledging our sins and failings . . .

Prayer

Lord Jesus, you are the true bread come down from heaven for the life of the world. In gratitude for this life-giving bread, which is the Word of God made flesh, we pray. **Amen.**

Gospel   **John 6:24-35**

When the crowd saw that neither Jesus nor his disciples were there, they themselves got into boats and came to Capernaum looking for Jesus. And when they found him across the sea they said to him, "Rabbi, when did you get here?" Jesus answered them and said, "Amen, amen, I say to you, you are looking for me not because you saw signs but because you ate the loaves and were filled. Do not work for food that perishes but for the food that endures for eternal life, which the Son of Man will give you. For on him the Father, God, has set his seal." So they said to him, "What can we do to accomplish the works of God?" Jesus answered and said to them, "This is the work of God, that you believe in the one he sent." So they said to him, "What sign can you do, that we may see and believe in you? What can you do? Our ancestors ate manna in the desert, as it is written: / *He gave them bread from heaven to eat.*" / So Jesus said to them, "Amen, amen, I say to you, it was not Moses who gave the bread from heaven; my Father gives you the true bread from heaven. For the bread of God is that which comes down from heaven and gives life to the world."

So they said to him, "Sir, give us this bread always." Jesus said to them, "I am the bread of life; whoever comes to me will never hunger, and whoever believes in me will never thirst."

Brief Silence

For Reflection

The day after the "multiplication of the loaves" the people were still seeking Jesus and found him in Capernaum. He admonishes them to seek not perishable food but the food of everlasting life. They only need to believe in him. But the people demand a sign similar to Moses providing manna in the desert. Jesus reminds them that it was not Moses, but the Father who gives "true bread from heaven." Jesus' addition of the word "true" is significant. In a double entendre, Jesus says that the true bread "comes down from heaven and gives life to the world." This sets the stage for his claim at the conclusion of the reading, that Jesus himself is the Bread of Life.

This is a remarkable teaching, for Jesus refers to himself as having come down from heaven. Essentially, this is a teaching reflecting the prologue of John's gospel, "In the beginning was the Word, / and the Word was with God" (1:1) and "the Word became flesh" (1:14). No other gospel makes such a claim. Johannine theology is Christology. The true bread from heaven that gives eternal life is none other than Jesus himself, the Word of God made flesh.

✦ What difference does the Eucharist make in my life that could not be fulfilled by other forms of prayer?

Brief Silence

Prayer

You have done great things for us, O Lord; rejoicing in the many blessings you have given us, we come to you with these prayers, confident, in faith, that you will hear them. In Jesus' name, we pray. **Amen.**

To prepare ourselves to celebrate this sacrament of the Bread of Life, let us ask God's forgiveness for our sins and failings . . .

Prayer

Lord Jesus, you are the Bread of Life, come down from heaven. This bread is your flesh, given to us sacramentally in the Eucharist. Inspire our faith with this knowledge and promise from you, that, having consumed this bread, we may have eternal life. **Amen.**

Gospel   **John 6:41-51**

The Jews murmured about Jesus because he said, "I am the bread that came down from heaven," and they said, "Is this not Jesus, the son of Joseph? Do we not know his father and mother? Then how can he say, 'I have come down from heaven'?" Jesus answered and said to them, "Stop murmuring among yourselves. No one can come to me unless the Father who sent me draw him, and I will raise him on the last day. It is written in the prophets: / *They shall all be taught by God.* / Everyone who listens to my Father and learns from him comes to me. Not that anyone has seen the Father except the one who is from God; he has seen the Father. Amen, amen, I say to you, whoever believes has eternal life. I am the bread of life. Your ancestors ate the manna in the desert, but they died; this is the bread that comes down from heaven so that one may eat it and not die. I am the living bread that came down from heaven; whoever eats this bread will live forever; and the bread that I will give is my flesh for the life of the world."

Brief Silence

For Reflection

In the gospel reading from last week the people wanted Jesus to give them a sign like the manna in the desert. In response Jesus claimed that he was the Bread of Life come down from heaven. This week he goes even further. He quotes Isaiah: "They shall all be taught by God." Both he and the crowds understood the meaning. He was placing himself on par with God or, rather, even equating himself with God. This was becoming too much. Rather than back down, Jesus goes another step further. The bread he gives is his very flesh.

With Jesus' willingness to go one step further followed by another and yet another, we will not be surprised to learn that many of his followers will abandon him. What he was teaching and preaching was beyond credibility. This upstart preacher from Galilee, whose father was somebody known in the community, was delusional if he claimed he came down from heaven as true bread, which is his very flesh. Somebody preaching that today would likely be ridiculed and summarily dismissed, which is what will ultimately happen to Jesus.

✦ How are we a "eucharistic" church?

Brief Silence

Prayer

Father of mercy, we place these prayers before you. As you have become bread for us, make us bread for one another; as your Spirit instills in us your love and peace, let us mirror that love and peace to one another. We offer these prayers in the name of Jesus, the Bread of Life. **Amen.**

With the faith and trust of Mary, let us place our hearts before God, confident of his mercy and forgiveness . . .

Prayer

Lord God Almighty, Mary proclaimed your greatness in her *Magnificat*. Her image of your kingdom inspires us still. Give us the courage to enact her vision, animated by the same Spirit that animated her Son. **Amen.**

Gospel   **Luke 1:39-56 (At the Mass during the Day)**

Mary set out and traveled to the hill country in haste to a town of Judah, where she entered the house of Zechariah and greeted Elizabeth. When Elizabeth heard Mary's greeting, the infant leaped in her womb, and Elizabeth, filled with the Holy Spirit, cried out in a loud voice and said, "Blessed are you among women, and blessed is the fruit of your womb. And how does this happen to me, that the mother of my Lord should come to me? For at the moment the sound of your greeting reached my ears, the infant in my womb leaped for joy. Blessed are you who believed that what was spoken to you by the Lord would be fulfilled."

And Mary said: / "My soul proclaims the greatness of the Lord; / my spirit rejoices in God my Savior / for he has looked with favor on his lowly servant. / From this day all generations will call me blessed: / the Almighty has done great things for me / and holy is his Name. / He has mercy on those who fear him / in every generation. / He has shown the strength of his arm, / and has scattered the proud in their conceit. / He has cast down the mighty from their thrones, / and has lifted up the lowly. / He has filled the hungry with good things, / and the rich he has sent away empty. / He has come to the help of his servant Israel / for he has remembered his promise of mercy, / the promise he made to our fathers, / to Abraham and his children forever."

Mary remained with her about three months and then returned to her home.

Brief Silence

For Reflection

The canticle we hear in today's gospel reading is from Mary. It is also referred to as the *Magnificat* ("magnifies"), which is the first word in the Latin translation. She utters this upon hearing her cousin Elizabeth state that the infant (John) in her womb "leapt for joy." Mary proclaims a profound reversal of fortune. The rulers are thrown down from their thrones and the lowly are lifted up. The rich are sent away empty while the hungry receive their fill. Mary sounds like she was quite a preacher! Is there any wonder where Jesus received his own sense of justice and identification with those who were on the bottom rungs of society? These messages were imbibed by the young Jesus and we hear their echo in his own preaching as an adult. The worldly standards do not apply with God. An upheaval is about to take place. For those at the top of society they are a warning shot across the bow. For those heretofore shut out of privilege, these words are hope that God has heard their cry. This message sets the stage for Jesus' own ministry, and ultimately ours.

✦ What single image of Mary's Magnificat most resonates with me?

Brief Silence

Prayer

O God, hear the prayers we offer. May Mary's prayer, the gift of a mother's love, be our joy; may her faith, the humble response of her generous heart, inspire us to live lives worthy of your promise. We ask these things in the name of your Son, Mary's child, Jesus Christ. **Amen.**

Trusting in the constant forgiveness of God, let us call to mind our sins and failings . . .

Prayer

Jesus, Bread of Life, you give us your very self for our nourishment, for your flesh is true food and your blood true drink. With eyes of faith we see you in the Eucharist. May our consumption of your sacramental feast lead us to eternal life. **Amen.**

Gospel   John 6:51-58

Jesus said to the crowds: "I am the living bread that came down from heaven; whoever eats this bread will live forever; and the bread that I will give is my flesh for the life of the world."

The Jews quarreled among themselves, saying, "How can this man give us his flesh to eat?" Jesus said to them, "Amen, amen, I say to you, unless you eat the flesh of the Son of Man and drink his blood, you do not have life within you. Whoever eats my flesh and drinks my blood has eternal life, and I will raise him on the last day. For my flesh is true food, and my blood is true drink. Whoever eats my flesh and drinks my blood remains in me and I in him. Just as the living Father sent me and I have life because of the Father, so also the one who feeds on me will have life because of me. This is the bread that came down from heaven. Unlike your ancestors who ate and still died, whoever eats this bread will live forever."

Brief Silence

For Reflection

Today's gospel begins with the same verse that formed the conclusion of last week's gospel. That line last week was the pinnacle of a series of "ratcheting it up" on Jesus' behalf. This week, that line merely sets the stage for Jesus' going even further. His opponents immediately questioned Jesus' meaning about his flesh being true food. In reply Jesus does not apologize for an apparent misunderstanding. He does not say that his image was only a metaphor, not meant to be taken literally. Instead, he adds the term "blood" to flesh and continues with his preaching to mean that unless someone consumes his flesh *and blood* there is no life in that person. And so that there is no room for misunderstanding, he claims his flesh is true food and his blood true drink.

We will not be surprised to see the puzzlement and anger on the part of his opponents grow. Jesus is not backing down; he is not backing away. He continues to raise the stakes and make claims that sound more and more baffling to the crowds and to many others. Only with eyes of faith can we, like his disciples, accept this teaching. Many more are those who will walk away bewildered.

✦ Have I ever participated in some sharing of food or drink that I found to be a meaningful experience of "communion"?

Brief Silence

Prayer

With gratitude and hope, we offer these prayers to you, Father of grace, trusting in your loving mercy and providence. We offer these prayers to you in the name of Jesus, the Bread of Life. **Amen.**

To prepare ourselves to celebrate these sacred mysteries, let us confess our sins and faults, humbly seeking the mercy of God . . .

Prayer

Lord God, you sent your Son Jesus as the Bread of Life, come down from heaven. You also gave us the faith to believe in him. May we be humble with the gift of faith, never using it against another, but only as a source of joy and happiness. **Amen.**

Gospel   **John 6:60-69**

Many of Jesus' disciples who were listening said, "This saying is hard; who can accept it?" Since Jesus knew that his disciples were murmuring about this, he said to them, "Does this shock you? What if you were to see the Son of Man ascending to where he was before? It is the spirit that gives life, while the flesh is of no avail. The words I have spoken to you are Spirit and life. But there are some of you who do not believe." Jesus knew from the beginning the ones who would not believe and the one who would betray him. And he said, "For this reason I have told you that no one can come to me unless it is granted him by my Father."

As a result of this, many of his disciples returned to their former way of life and no longer accompanied him. Jesus then said to the Twelve, "Do you also want to leave?" Simon Peter answered him, "Master, to whom shall we go? You have the words of eternal life. We have come to believe and are convinced that you are the Holy One of God."

Brief Silence

For Reflection

Today is the fifth and final Sunday of our reading from John 6, the second longest chapter in the New Testament (Luke 1 is the longest). The church gives us five Sundays with this chapter precisely because of its profound eucharistic theology. What began with the multiplication of the loaves ends the following day with nearly all of his disciples abandoning him and returning to their former way of life precisely because of this "hard" saying, the consumption of Jesus' very flesh and blood.

Jesus then asks the Twelve if they too will leave. He was not going to change his teaching to attract the crowds. Instead, he would teach what he knew to be true, for his words were Spirit and life. Jesus knows that nobody can come to him, can believe in him, unless it is granted by the Father. We cannot come to Jesus unless we are given the gift of faith. Only if that special gift is granted by the Father will one believe. All the arguments, discussions, proofs, demonstrations, blog posts, and talks cannot guarantee faith. It is a gift given not by us, but by God the Father.

✦ What "sayings" of Jesus do I find especially hard to accept?

Brief Silence

Prayer

Gracious God, hear our prayers. Instill in us your Spirit so that we may carry on in the certainty of your Son's words of spirit and life. In his name, we pray. **Amen.**

Confident of God's constant mercy and forgiveness, let us call to mind our sins and failings . . .

Prayer

Lord Jesus Christ, you came into the world and taught your disciples the meaning of true faith. May we be inspired by your teaching to place our focus not on externals but on the fundamental reason for the externals. **Amen.**

Gospel   **Mark 7:1-8, 14-15, 21-23**

When the Pharisees with some scribes who had come from Jerusalem gathered around Jesus, they observed that some of his disciples ate their meals with unclean, that is, unwashed, hands.—For the Pharisees and, in fact, all Jews, do not eat without carefully washing their hands, keeping the tradition of the elders. And on coming from the marketplace they do not eat without purifying themselves. And there are many other things that they have traditionally observed, the purification of cups and jugs and kettles and beds.—So the Pharisees and scribes questioned him, "Why do your disciples not follow the tradition of the elders but instead eat a meal with unclean hands?" He responded, "Well did Isaiah prophesy about you hypocrites, as it is written: / *This people honors me with their lips, / but their hearts are far from me; / in vain do they worship me, / teaching as doctrines human precepts.* / You disregard God's commandment but cling to human tradition."

He summoned the crowd again and said to them, "Hear me, all of you, and understand. Nothing that enters one from outside can defile that person; but the things that come out from within are what defile.

"From within people, from their hearts, come evil thoughts, unchastity, theft, murder, adultery, greed, malice, deceit, licentiousness, envy, blasphemy, arrogance, folly. All these evils come from within and they defile."

Brief Silence

For Reflection

Today we return to the Gospel of Mark after a five-week trip through John 6. In some ways Mark may seem to be familiar territory after the theological digression through the bread of life discourse and its antecedents. There are some explanatory notes in the gospel today that seem intended for a non-Jewish audience. Mark tells us about some Jewish practices of the time that would have been unfamiliar to the readers of his gospel. For this reason among others the audience would have been sizably, if not majority, Gentile. So quickly (a few decades) after Jesus' death and resurrection the gospel message moved beyond the Jewish soil where it first took root, and grew among Gentiles. It's almost like a cultivated ivy that leaped over a natural boundary to take root beyond the garden.

With this gospel reading it is as though we are listening in to one side of a family feud. We hear the early Christians' take on their elder sibling's faith. Not surprisingly, the Christians were critical of Jewish practices, claiming they missed the point. But it would be a misreading to see this only as a history lesson. The practices criticized in this gospel are perilously close to those of any religious person. There is a strong temptation to believe that we, by our actions and good deeds, make ourselves worthy of God. It can be easy to focus on the externals of religious practice and miss the point of religion. It can be easy to focus on ritual washing, or any ritual, and miss the deeper, more meaningful action indicated by the ritual.

✦ What's the difference between one's faith and one's religion?

Brief Silence

Prayer

May your word of life and love "take root" in our hearts, O God, so that these prayers we offer may become a harvest of justice and peace for all our brothers and sisters. In Jesus' name, we pray. **Amen.**

Let us begin our celebration of the Eucharist by asking the God of mercy and healing to forgive us our sins and restore us to hope . . .

Prayer

Lord Jesus, doer of mighty deeds, you opened the ears of the deaf and restored the outcast. Give us the same spirit so that we who are deaf to your words may hear, and that those who are marginalized may be brought into the fold. **Amen.**

Gospel   **Mark 7:31-37**

Again Jesus left the district of Tyre and went by way of Sidon to the Sea of Galilee, into the district of the Decapolis. And people brought to him a deaf man who had a speech impediment and begged him to lay his hand on him. He took him off by himself away from the crowd. He put his finger into the man's ears and, spitting, touched his tongue; then he looked up to heaven and groaned, and said to him, *"Ephphatha!"*—that is, "Be opened!"— And immediately the man's ears were opened, his speech impediment was removed, and he spoke plainly. He ordered them not to tell anyone. But the more he ordered them not to, the more they proclaimed it. They were exceedingly astonished and they said, "He has done all things well. He makes the deaf hear and the mute speak."

Brief Silence

For Reflection

How might today's unique Markan story be portrayed in artwork? Can we imagine Jesus putting his finger in another person's ear? Or Jesus spitting and touching the person's tongue, groaning in a foreign language? Even so, that's precisely what the gospel tells us happened. And the Aramaic term preserved in the Greek New Testament, *Ephphatha* is in the imperative singular form and clearly means, "Be opened."

Perhaps we are not surprised to hear that in the early centuries after Jesus' death and resurrection many thought of him as a magician. But of course Jesus was not a magician. His mighty deeds were ushering in the kingdom of God. His actions were being done "by the finger of God" rather than by a magic wand. The mighty deeds of Jesus were about restoration, healing, and wholeness. Those on the margins, those outcast, and those who were relegated to a kind of second-class citizenship on account of physical ailments were healed, made whole, and thereby restored to the community.

✦ When have I been especially blessed by another person's gift of simple listening?

Brief Silence

Prayer

Open our eyes and ears and hearts to your Spirit, O God, that everything we do and every moment you give us may speak of your loving presence in our world and bring to joyful completion these prayers we offer to you in the name of your Son, Jesus the compassionate healer. **Amen.**

As we prepare to celebrate these sacred mysteries, let us call to mind our sins and failings . . .

Prayer

Lord Jesus, you were proclaimed as "Christ" by Peter and yet he misunderstood the meaning of that title. Give us the insight regarding your true identity, so that we may come to a deeper understanding of your presence in our lives. **Amen.**

Gospel   **Mark 8:27-35**

Jesus and his disciples set out for the villages of Caesarea Philippi. Along the way he asked his disciples, "Who do people say that I am?" They said in reply, "John the Baptist, others Elijah, still others one of the prophets." And he asked them, "But who do you say that I am?" Peter said to him in reply, "You are the Christ." Then he warned them not to tell anyone about him.

He began to teach them that the Son of Man must suffer greatly and be rejected by the elders, the chief priests, and the scribes, and be killed, and rise after three days. He spoke this openly. Then Peter took him aside and began to rebuke him. At this he turned around and, looking at his disciples, rebuked Peter and said, "Get behind me, Satan. You are thinking not as God does, but as human beings do."

He summoned the crowd with his disciples and said to them, "Whoever wishes to come after me must deny himself, take up his cross, and follow me. For whoever wishes to save his life will lose it, but whoever loses his life for my sake and that of the gospel will save it."

Brief Silence

For Reflection

Jesus tells the crowds and his disciples that to be one of his followers one must be ready to "take up his cross, and follow me." Jesus does not need admirers, but he does want followers. And those followers might get hurt. In fact, they are told to take up their cross. The Christian life is not likened to a recliner, but a cross. As founder and leader of this movement, Jesus foretells his own suffering and death. This is met with incredulity on Peter's part so much so that he rebukes Jesus! It seems Peter misunderstood the implication of his own confession. This should be a warning for us too who confess Jesus as Christ, Lord, or any other title. Our own understanding of who Jesus is, and what he is to do, may not conform to the reality of who Jesus is, and what he is to do. Though Peter had been one of the first disciples called by Jesus, and had witnessed his ministry up to this point, he still misunderstood.

This story of "Peter's confession" forms the centerpiece of the Gospel of Mark. Not until the death of Jesus will another human being (the centurion) recognize Jesus as Son of God, the second title of Jesus from Mark 1:1. This becomes a literary way of expressing Jesus' identity. He is Christ, and he will suffer and die. Only after doing so can he be fully understood as Son of God.

✦ What is the most difficult and challenging cross that I carry? Has it ever been a means of resurrection in my life?

Brief Silence

Prayer

Gracious God, hear the prayers we lift up to you. By your grace, may we follow your Son by "crucifying" our self-interests and wants and take up our crosses to bring the life of his resurrection into our world. We offer these prayers in the name of Jesus, the Son of God and Christ. **Amen.**

Let us place our hearts and spirits in the presence of God, seeking his forgiveness for our sins . . .

Prayer

Lord Jesus, you taught your disciples that servanthood is greater than being the master, and that the true leader is the servant of others. Allow that teaching to inform our spirituality today so that we might become disciples following in your footsteps. **Amen.**

Gospel   Mark 9:30-37

Jesus and his disciples left from there and began a journey through Galilee, but he did not wish anyone to know about it. He was teaching his disciples and telling them, "The Son of Man is to be handed over to men and they will kill him, and three days after his death the Son of Man will rise." But they did not understand the saying, and they were afraid to question him.

They came to Capernaum and, once inside the house, he began to ask them, "What were you arguing about on the way?" But they remained silent. They had been discussing among themselves on the way who was the greatest. Then he sat down, called the Twelve, and said to them, "If anyone wishes to be first, he shall be the last of all and the servant of all." Taking a child, he placed it in their midst, and putting his arms around it, he said to them, "Whoever receives one child such as this in my name, receives me; and whoever receives me, receives not me but the One who sent me."

Brief Silence

For Reflection

The disciples are examples for us in so many ways, but today their example might not be what we expect. Here not only do they misunderstand Jesus (again) but they are afraid to ask him any questions. They are arguing amongst themselves. So Jesus turns the table and questions them. He wants them to tell him what they were arguing about. This almost sounds like a family squabble among the children where the parent has to step in and put a foot down. Perhaps like petulant children called on the carpet, the disciples remain silent. They do not have an answer for Jesus. Is this the way the disciples really acted? Are these the saints we revere? Are their actions worthy of emulation?

Jesus then teaches the Twelve about leadership and being counted as the first. The leader is to be the servant. This upends ancient ideas and certainly modern thinking about being "number one." Power, riches, and authority, both in antiquity and now, are often used to amass more. But for the Christian it is to be different. For those who desire to be first, the greatest, the best, they are to be the last, the least, the servant of all.

✦ Do I know of individuals whose humility has led them to accomplish great things for others?

Brief Silence

Prayer

Hear our prayers, O God. May we possess the spirit of humility and generosity of your Son that enables us to be the means for making possible what we have asked of you. In Jesus' name, we pray. **Amen.**

The Lord of mercy has gathered us together at his table. Let us begin by acknowledging our sins and failings and, through his mercy, celebrate these sacred mysteries in his peace . . .

Prayer

Jesus Christ, you are the great Master, Teacher of wisdom. Your mission was extensive and inclusive. Give us the same spirit of inclusivity when we seek to teach in your name. **Amen.**

Gospel   Mark 9:38-43, 45, 47-48

At that time, John said to Jesus, "Teacher, we saw someone driving out demons in your name, and we tried to prevent him because he does not follow us." Jesus replied, "Do not prevent him. There is no one who performs a mighty deed in my name who can at the same time speak ill of me. For whoever is not against us is for us. Anyone who gives you a cup of water to drink because you belong to Christ, amen, I say to you, will surely not lose his reward.

"Whoever causes one of these little ones who believe in me to sin, it would be better for him if a great millstone were put around his neck and he were thrown into the sea. If your hand causes you to sin, cut it off. It is better for you to enter into life maimed than with two hands to go into Gehenna, into the unquenchable fire. And if your foot causes you to sin, cut if off. It is better for you to enter into life crippled than with two feet to be thrown into Gehenna. And if your eye causes you to sin, pluck it out. Better for you to enter into the kingdom of God with one eye than with two eyes to be thrown into Gehenna, where 'their worm does not die, and the fire is not quenched.'"

Brief Silence

For Reflection

Today the disciples, in their continuing streak of misunderstanding, come to Jesus with some news. It's as though they are tattling, "We saw someone doing something in your name, but he's not in our group so we stopped him." Jesus responds with the equivalent of, "No one likes a tattletale." He then makes a claim that can be described as "big tent" Christianity, in saying that "whoever is not against us is for us." The double negative "not against" is significant, and seems to be a rather low bar. If simply not being against is the equivalent of being "for" there seems to be hope!

Yet, this rather low-bar admonition is followed immediately by a stern and disturbing warning: Causing a little one to sin is worthy of death. What then follows are a series of prophetic hyperbole intended to make the point that the kingdom of God is worth any price. Lopping off a body part that causes one to sin is better than losing eternal life. The early church recognized these commands concerning self-maiming as hyperbole and did not take them literally. These are warnings to sever any relationship that causes sin. The kingdom of God is the ultimate prize worth any price.

✦ How does faith become "elitist"?

Brief Silence

Prayer

May our offering of these prayers, O God, inspire us to be about the work of reconciliation and justice, of mercy and peace, entrusted to us by your Son, Christ Jesus, in whose name we pray. **Amen.**

As we prepare to celebrate these sacred mysteries, let us seek the forgiveness of God for our sins and failings . . .

Prayer

God Almighty, you gave marriage to the human race as a sign of your love and fidelity. May all of our relationships live up to the ideal. But when they do not, grant us your spirit of wisdom and prudence. **Amen.**

Gospel   **Mark 10:2-16**

The Pharisees approached Jesus and asked, "Is it lawful for a husband to divorce his wife?" They were testing him. He said to them in reply, "What did Moses command you?" They replied, "Moses permitted a husband to write a bill of divorce and dismiss her." But Jesus told them, "Because of the hardness of your hearts he wrote you this commandment. But from the beginning of creation, *God made them male and female. For this reason a man shall leave his father and mother and be joined to his wife, and the two shall become one flesh.* So they are no longer two but one flesh. Therefore what God has joined together, no human being must separate." In the house the disciples again questioned Jesus about this. He said to them, "Whoever divorces his wife and marries another commits adultery against her; and if she divorces her husband and marries another, she commits adultery."

And people were bringing children to him that he might touch them, but the disciples rebuked them. When Jesus saw this he became indignant and said to them, "Let the children come to me; do not prevent them, for the kingdom of God belongs to such

as these. Amen, I say to you, whoever does not accept the kingdom of God like a child will not enter it." Then he embraced them
and blessed them, placing his hands on them.

Brief Silence

For Reflection

In today's gospel, rather than offer a flexible interpretation of the
Mosaic law concerning divorce, Jesus doubles down. He tells the
audience that the only reason Moses even permitted divorce was
because of human stubbornness. In actuality, Jesus says, in quoting Genesis, "what God has joined together, / no human being
must separate." He goes even further (thus the doubling down)
and makes a startling statement that the man who divorces his
wife and marries another commits adultery. And for parity's sake,
he says that the woman who divorces her husband and marries
another commits adultery. In any case, this prohibition was, and
remains, extreme. We can see evidence that the early church considered this extreme because Matthew's Gospel   which
uses Mark as a source) already amends the prohibition and makes
an exception for divorce in cases of unlawful marriage, sometimes
erroneously translated as "sexual immorality" (see Matt 19:9).

As adults, we approach faith with a certain maturity. Rather
than accept at face value each and every saying in the Bible, we
discern the meaning of the text in a community of faith.

✦ How does a covenant relationship differ from a contract
arrangement?

Brief Silence

Prayer

To you who are the Father of creation, the Source of love and
peace, and the Protector of the poor and lost, we offer these
prayers for all our brothers and sisters. Hear and grant these
prayers we offer, O God, in the name of your Son, Jesus the Christ.
Amen.

As we prepare to celebrate these sacred mysteries, let us acknowledge our sins, seeking the mercy of God and the forgiveness of one another . . .

Prayer

Jesus, you call disciples in every time and place and ask that they follow you. Give us the sole dedication to following you also, that we may give up anything that would hinder us along the path. In your name we pray. **Amen.**

Gospel   **Mark 10:17-30 (or Mark 10:17-27)**

As Jesus was setting out on a journey, a man ran up, knelt down before him, and asked him, "Good teacher, what must I do to inherit eternal life?" Jesus answered him, "Why do you call me good? No one is good but God alone. You know the commandments: *You shall not kill; you shall not commit adultery; you shall not steal; you shall not bear false witness; you shall not defraud; honor your father and your mother.*" He replied and said to him, "Teacher, all of these I have observed from my youth." Jesus, looking at him, loved him and said to him, "You are lacking in one thing. Go, sell what you have, and give to the poor and you will have treasure in heaven; then come, follow me." At that statement his face fell, and he went away sad, for he had many possessions.

Jesus looked around and said to his disciples, "How hard it is for those who have wealth to enter the kingdom of God!" The disciples were amazed at his words. So Jesus again said to them in reply, "Children, how hard it is to enter the kingdom of God! It is easier for a camel to pass through the eye of a needle than for one who is rich to enter the kingdom of God." They were exceedingly astonished and said among themselves, "Then who can be saved?" Jesus looked at them and said, "For human beings it is impossible, but not for God. All things are possible for God." Peter began to say to him, "We have given up everything and followed you." Jesus said, "Amen, I say to you, there is no one who has given up house or brothers or sisters or mother or father or children or lands for my sake and for the sake of the gospel who will not receive a hundred times more now in this present age: houses and brothers and sisters and mothers and children and lands, with persecutions, and eternal life in the age to come."

Brief Silence

For Reflection

How many of us have wished to meet Jesus? Or perhaps, like today's gospel, simply to have been able to ask Jesus a question? The man who does receives a loving look from Jesus. It even sounds like Jesus admired the goodwill of this person, who desired eternal life. The questioner has followed all of the commandments. He is in right standing with the law. But he feels there is more. Jesus, in turn, gives him a challenge that he gave to no other person. Namely, Jesus tells him to sell his many possessions, give the proceeds to the poor, and then follow him.

Instead, the man clung to his possessions. He loved them more than he wanted to follow Jesus. And this is a warning shot to all who would follow Jesus. Whom or what do we love more? Possessions? Jesus? Jesus wants a complete and total commitment of the individual. And with this man, Jesus seems to know that for him, the one thing holding him back is his wealth. So Jesus invites him to discard it. What does Jesus invite us to discard?

✦ Has my possession of something of value ever turned out to be an unhappy, unsatisfying experience?

Brief Silence

Prayer

Hear these prayers we offer to you, O God. Open our hearts to embrace the spirit of your Son's Gospel, so that we may bring to fulfillment your kingdom in this time and place of ours. In Jesus' name, we pray. **Amen.**

Let us begin our celebration of the Eucharist by placing our hearts before God, asking for his mercy for our sins and failings . . .

Prayer

Jesus, we long to be near you, and to have you do what we ask. Give us a humble spirit so that we may be of service to others as you were in your earthly ministry. **Amen.**

Gospel   Mark 10:35-45 (or Mark 10:42-45)

James and John, the sons of Zebedee, came to Jesus and said to him, "Teacher, we want you to do for us whatever we ask of you." He replied, "What do you wish me to do for you?" They answered him, "Grant that in your glory we may sit one at your right and the other at your left." Jesus said to them, "You do not know what you are asking. Can you drink the cup that I drink or be baptized with the baptism with which I am baptized?" They said to him, "We can." Jesus said to them, "The cup that I drink, you will drink, and with the baptism with which I am baptized, you will be baptized; but to sit at my right or at my left is not mine to give but is for those for whom it has been prepared." When the ten heard this, they became indignant at James and John. Jesus summoned them and said to them, "You know that those who are recognized as rulers over the Gentiles lord it over them, and their great ones make their authority over them felt. But it shall not be so among you. Rather, whoever wishes to be great among you will be your servant; whoever wishes to be first among you will be the slave of all. For the Son of Man did not come to be served but to serve and to give his life as a ransom for many."

Brief Silence

For Reflection

Human nature being what it is, two men, brothers in the case of today's gospel, are angling to get a better deal. They speak with Jesus on their own, in private. Their rather bold statement, "we want you to do for us whatever we ask of you" is met with open receptivity on Jesus' part. With patience, Jesus asks the brothers, "What do you wish me to do for you?" What would be our own reply to Jesus at that moment? His question is wide open. For the brothers, they want glory, to sit at Jesus' side in his kingdom. They still imagine that Jesus will be a powerful earthly King, ruling over an independent and free Jewish people. But as Jesus did with Peter after Peter proclaimed him the Messiah, he corrects James and John's misconception. Jesus told Peter that the Son of Man would suffer and ultimately die. He will invite the sons of Zebedee to do the same by asking if they can drink the cup that he drinks. When the brothers seek glory, and a seat at either side of Jesus, they do not realize that they are thereby accepting suffering.

✦ Have I ever had to confront another's ambition or arrogance, similar to the attitude of James and John in today's gospel?

Brief Silence

Prayer

Hear these prayers, O God. By your mercy and grace, may we create your kingdom here and now by embracing your Son's attitude of humble and selfless service to all. In Jesus' name, we pray. **Amen.**

Let us begin our celebration of these sacred mysteries by humbly asking God's healing mercy for our sins and failings . . .

Prayer

Lord Jesus, worker of wonders, you make the blind see. Give sight to those of us blind to what we do not see. Give us the eyes of faith so that we may minister in your name to the needs in our world. **Amen.**

Gospel   Mark 10:46-52

As Jesus was leaving Jericho with his disciples and a sizable crowd, Bartimaeus, a blind man, the son of Timaeus, sat by the roadside begging. On hearing that it was Jesus of Nazareth, he began to cry out and say, "Jesus, son of David, have pity on me." And many rebuked him, telling him to be silent. But he kept calling out all the more, "Son of David, have pity on me." Jesus stopped and said, "Call him." So they called the blind man, saying to him, "Take courage; get up, Jesus is calling you." He threw aside his cloak, sprang up, and came to Jesus. Jesus said to him in reply, "What do you want me to do for you?" The blind man replied to him, "Master, I want to see." Jesus told him, "Go your way; your faith has saved you." Immediately he received his sight and followed him on the way.

Brief Silence

For Reflection

The Gospel of Mark introduces us to a variety of characters not seen elsewhere or even mentioned again in the New Testament. Bartimaeus, the blind man, is one such example. From the way the story is told, Bartimaeus certainly had heard of Jesus, for upon learning that he was on the road, Bartimaeus immediately cries out. But he is shut down. In an exchange reminiscent of Jesus' interaction with James and John last week, Jesus asks him point-blank, "What do you want me to do for you?" We recall how James and John answered. They wanted glory. But Bartimaeus responds differently. He simply wants to see. For him, not one of the Twelve, not one of the chosen from the beginning, there is no grasping for power, glory, or authority. Bartimaeus merely wants to be made whole.

Jesus' response and Bartimaeus's healing is immediate and simultaneous. His sight is restored and he follows Jesus. Perhaps surprisingly, we never hear of Bartimaeus again. He is now a true disciple, a follower of Jesus. And his faith response to Jesus is a model for us, perhaps even a better model than the brothers James and John.

✦ What do I want the Lord to do for me?

Brief Silence

Prayer

Lord of light, open our eyes to the light of your love so that we may bring to reality the prayers and hopes that you alone see in the depths of our hearts. We make these prayers to you in the name of Jesus, the healing Christ. **Amen.**

With joy and thanksgiving we gather to celebrate the supper of the Lamb of God, sacrificed for us. Let us begin our Eucharist on this All Saints' Day by seeking God's mercy for our sins and failings . . .

Prayer

God Almighty, you called us to yourself, to be dedicated to you in this world. May we be worthy of our calling, followers of your Son, and driven by his Spirit. **Amen.**

Gospel   **Matt 5:1-12a**

When Jesus saw the crowds, he went up the mountain, and after he had sat down, his disciples came to him. He began to teach them, saying: / "Blessed are the poor in spirit, / for theirs is the Kingdom of heaven. / Blessed are they who mourn, / for they will be comforted. / Blessed are the meek, / for they will inherit the land. / Blessed are they who hunger and thirst for righteousness, / for they will be satisfied. / Blessed are the merciful, / for they will be shown mercy. / Blessed are the clean of heart, / for they will see God. / Blessed are the peacemakers, / for they will be called children of God. / Blessed are they who are persecuted for the sake of righteousness, / for theirs is the Kingdom of heaven. / Blessed are you when they insult you and persecute you and utter every kind of evil against you falsely because of me. Rejoice and be glad, for your reward will be great in heaven."

Brief Silence

For Reflection

Saint Paul called the recipients of his letters "saints," not in the sense that they were "holy rollers," but rather that they were called by God to be set apart in the world. They were dedicated to God.

And perhaps there can be no better gospel reading on a day that celebrates all the saints than the Beatitudes of Matthew. Some church fathers called the Beatitudes a self-portrait of Jesus. Jesus was poor in spirit. He mourned. He was meek; he hungered and thirsted for righteousness and was persecuted for its sake. Yet he remained merciful, clean of heart, and a peacemaker. In doing so, Jesus gave a model for what discipleship should look like, as a disciple follows Jesus. If we are to follow him, the Beatitudes should not only be a self-portrait of Jesus, but a portrait of us too. Of course, living the Beatitudes is a tall order. But in so doing we will find ourselves to be the saints we are called to be. We will be worthy of the name Paul gives to his Christian communities, for we will be dedicated to God, set apart in the world.

✦ What is the most intimidating or daunting challenge of becoming a "saint"?

Brief Silence

Prayer

Father, we join our prayers this day with the eternal praise of the blessed in heaven. May we possess your grace to realize your kingdom of compassion and in this world as we await its fulfillment in the next. We offer our prayer to you in the name of your Son, Jesus the Lord. **Amen.**

Let us begin our celebration of these sacred mysteries by seeking the mercy of God, who raises us up from our sin and despair to bring us into the light of his dwelling place . . .

Prayer

Lord Jesus, you promised the Father that you would not lose anything that the Father had given to you. We rest assured in that promise and it gives us hope that we will be reunited with you and all of our loved ones on the last day. **Amen.**

Gospel   **John 6:37-40**

Jesus said to the crowds: "Everything that the Father gives me will come to me, and I will not reject anyone who comes to me, because I came down from heaven not to do my own will but the will of the one who sent me. And this is the will of the one who sent me, that I should not lose anything of what he gave me, but that I should raise it on the last day. For this is the will of my Father, that everyone who sees the Son and believes in him may have eternal life, and I shall raise him on the last day."

Brief Silence

For Reflection

The word "soul" is polyvalent. It can mean almost anything to anyone. According to a 1979 Congregation for the Doctrine of the Faith document, "The Church affirms that a spiritual element survives and subsists after death, an element endowed with consciousness and will, so that the 'human self' subsists. To designate this element, the Church uses the word 'soul,' the accepted term in the usage of Scripture and Tradition" (Letter on Certain Questions Concerning Eschatology, 3). And so today we commemorate All Souls' Day, or perhaps, in light of the church's definition of "soul," All Human Selves Day. We are celebrating all those who have gone before us in faith. We commemorate "All the Faithful Departed."

How appropriate, then, that on this day we hear Jesus from John's gospel speaking about how his mission is not to lose anything the Father gave him. Jesus will raise them up. This promise is eternal and eschatological. It is eternal in that it was not meant for Jesus' generation only, but that the promise endures through the ages up to and including us. The promise is eschatological in that Jesus will raise those who have been given to him on the last day.

✦ What does the reality of death reveal about the nature of life?

Brief Silence

Prayer

Hear, O Lord, our prayers this day for our relatives and friends who have gone before us, marked with the sign of faith. We give you thanks for the blessing of their presence in our lives. We commend them to you again, consoled that you have made a place for them in your dwelling place and looking forward to that day when we take our places with them at your table in heaven. We make these prayers in the name of Jesus, the risen One. **Amen.**

Other gospel options for November 2:

Matthew 5:1-12a / Matthew 11:25-30 / Matthew 25:31-46 / Luke 7:11-17 / Luke 23:44-46, 50, 52-53; 24:1-6a / Luke 24:13-16, 28-35 / John 5:24-29 / John 6:51-58 / John 11:17-27 / John 11:32-45 / John 14:1-6

As we gather to celebrate these sacred mysteries, let us seek the mercy of God for our sins and failings . . .

Prayer

Lord God, you gave us the commandments so that we might have life. You sent your Son so that we might have everlasting life. Give us now the wisdom to live according to your commandments as taught by your Son so that our life might be full, and we shall have the promise of eternity. **Amen.**

Gospel   Mark 12:28b-34

One of the scribes came to Jesus and asked him, "Which is the first of all the commandments?" Jesus replied, "The first is this: *Hear, O Israel! The Lord our God is Lord alone! You shall love the Lord your God with all your heart, with all your soul, with all your mind, and with all your strength.* The second is this: *You shall love your neighbor as yourself.* There is no other commandment greater than these." The scribe said to him, "Well said, teacher. You are right in saying, 'He is One and there is no other than he.' And 'to love him with all your heart, with all your understanding, with all your strength, and to love your neighbor as yourself' is worth more than all burnt offerings and sacrifices." And when Jesus saw that he answered with understanding, he said to him, "You are not far from the kingdom of God." And no one dared to ask him any more questions.

Brief Silence

For Reflection

One of the scribes, one of those learned in the law and all things Jewish, came to Jesus with a deceptively simple question. "Which is the first of all the commandments?" Jesus' answer cleverly combines two commandments (Deut 6:4; Lev 19:18) to be the greatest. "There is no other commandment greater than these." In fact, though each commandment is in the Torah, scholars know of no other prophet or teacher prior to Jesus who had ever combined these two commandments in this way. There is nothing for the scribe to critique. He affirms and admiringly repeats Jesus' response, for which he is told, "You are not far from the kingdom of God." Jesus so embodies the law that no one else has the courage to ask him any questions.

But for us Christians, how is the Christian life summed up? By going to Mass on Sundays and holy days? By making First Fridays? By observing Lent? Or are those acts more akin to the burnt offerings and sacrifices prescribed by the law? Might there be something more foundational to the Christian life than even doctrines, creeds, holy days, or Lent? Perhaps Jesus' words are meant for us too. If only we love God and love our neighbor as ourselves.

✦ What is the most difficult personal need or want to put aside in order to "love your neighbor as yourself"?

Brief Silence

Prayer

Hear our prayer, O Lord, for all our brothers and sisters. Instill in us your Spirit of love to imitate the selfless humility of your Son so that we may realize your kingdom of compassion and peace in our own time and place. In Jesus' name, we pray. **Amen.**

Gathered by our Father in heaven to celebrate these sacred mysteries, let us seek his mercy and peace by calling to mind our sins . . .

Prayer

Good and gracious God, you give us every good thing. Give us too a generous spirit so that we may share the many gifts we have been given. In so doing, may we come to be like you—good, gracious, and generous. **Amen.**

Gospel   Mark 12:38-44 (or Mark 12:41-44)

In the course of his teaching Jesus said to the crowds, "Beware of the scribes, who like to go around in long robes and accept greetings in the marketplaces, seats of honor in synagogues, and places of honor at banquets. They devour the houses of widows and, as a pretext, recite lengthy prayers. They will receive a very severe condemnation."

He sat down opposite the treasury and observed how the crowd put money into the treasury. Many rich people put in large sums. A poor widow also came and put in two small coins worth a few cents. Calling his disciples to himself, he said to them, "Amen, I say to you, this poor widow put in more than all the other contributors to the treasury. For they have all contributed from their surplus wealth, but she, from her poverty, has contributed all she had, her whole livelihood."

Brief Silence

For Reflection

In the second vignette in today's gospel Jesus criticizes the rich, who give large sums to make a show, and to attract attention to their giving. Even though their gifts were large, and undoubtedly made a difference, these people gave from their excess. It was pocket change, not the milk money. The poor widow, she whose house is being devoured by the religious authorities, gives everything she has. In other words, they who had much gave little of what they had. She who had little gave everything she had.

What kind of givers are we? Do we give of ourselves or from our excess? Jesus' message is to give everything we have, without holding anything back. It's too easy to game the system, to make a show out of giving. But Jesus is speaking of something more profound. Rather than the annual fundraising appeal that each of us participate in, or charitable contributions that are a hallmark of Christianity, we are summoned by Jesus to give our entire selves. Rather than write a check equivalent to a family dinner at a restaurant, Jesus wants us entirely, without reservation.

✦ Have I ever met the "widow" of today's gospel?

Brief Silence

Prayer

O God, you know our needs before we know them ourselves. With trust in your constant love and providence, we ask you to hear these prayers we offer for the people who await your salvation in your Son, Jesus Christ, in whose name we pray. **Amen.**

With confidence and hope in God's mercy and peace, let us begin this celebration of the Eucharist by calling to mind our sins . . .

Prayer

Lord Jesus Christ, you taught your disciples that we do not know when the end will be. But we will all face our own personal deaths. May our faith in you assure us on that day, when we pass from this life to the next. **Amen.**

Gospel   Mark 13:24-32

Jesus said to his disciples: "In those days after that tribulation the sun will be darkened, and the moon will not give its light, and the stars will be falling from the sky, and the powers in the heavens will be shaken.

"And then they will see 'the Son of Man coming in the clouds' with great power and glory, and then he will send out the angels and gather his elect from the four winds, from the end of the earth to the end of the sky.

"Learn a lesson from the fig tree. When its branch becomes tender and sprouts leaves, you know that summer is near. In the same way, when you see these things happening, know that he is near, at the gates. Amen, I say to you, this generation will not pass away until all these things have taken place. Heaven and earth will pass away, but my words will not pass away.

"But of that day or hour, no one knows, neither the angels in heaven, nor the Son, but only the Father."

Brief Silence

For Reflection

Each age has had its share of true believers who maintain that the world was doomed, ready to be destroyed by God, raining down his fiery wrath on the heathens. In today's gospel perhaps the most significant line is at the end, when Jesus says, "But of that day or hour, no one knows, / neither the angels in heaven, nor the Son, but only the Father." Despite that rather stark, plain sentence, we have all undoubtedly heard some say, "Jesus says nobody knows the day or hour, but he doesn't say anything about the month or the year!" And then zany speculations start. Such interpretations miss the mark wildly.

Rather than worry about when the world will end, it might be more productive to wonder about my own personal end. That is, when will I die? How have I prepared myself for that eventual end? How have I lived my days knowing that nothing I accumulate on earth will be taken with me when I pass from this life? We know that we are definitely going to experience our own personal end, our own death. We are less likely to be here for the end of the world.

✦ What "signs" around me remind me of the brevity of life and the preciousness of time?

Brief Silence

Prayer

O God, you are the beginning and end of all things and seasons. Hear these prayers we offer in the hope of your mercy, as we live in joyful expectation of your eternal reign of peace. In Jesus' name, we pray. **Amen.**

The risen Christ, the King of the Universe, has called us to his table to celebrate the sacrament of his Body and Blood. Let us begin by seeking the forgiveness and peace of his kingdom by acknowledging our sins and failings . . .

Prayer

Lord Jesus, you are King of Kings and Lord of Lords, yet your kingdom is not of this world. By dying to our own selves may we be raised up on the last day to live in your kingdom where you reign forever and ever. **Amen.**

Gospel   John 18:33b-37

Pilate said to Jesus, "Are you the King of the Jews?" Jesus answered, "Do you say this on your own or have others told you about me?" Pilate answered, "I am not a Jew, am I? Your own nation and the chief priests handed you over to me. What have you done?" Jesus answered, "My kingdom does not belong to this world. If my kingdom did belong to this world, my attendants would be fighting to keep me from being handed over to the Jews. But as it is, my kingdom is not here." So Pilate said to him, "Then you are a king?" Jesus answered, "You say I am a king. For this I was born and for this I came into the world, to testify to the truth. Everyone who belongs to the truth listens to my voice."

Brief Silence

For Reflection

The gospel reading for today brings us into the scene between Jesus and Pilate. Of course, we know how it will end, ultimately with the crucifixion and the antagonizing sign proclaiming Jesus, "King." But here in the midst of the conversation we hear eternal questions that cause us to consider, "What is truth?" Jesus makes a straightforward claim, that he is a king, and he has been sent to testify to the truth. Pilate, vested with political authority, including the power to inflict capital punishment, is wrapped up in a semantic argument about the nature of truth. He doesn't see the incarnation of truth, the King of Kings, standing before his very eyes. And in Pilate's blindness, he will put to death Jesus as King of the Jews.

So the early Christians, and even us today, continue to proclaim Jesus as King. He is no mere figurehead. Instead, he shares the title with Yahweh, "great king over the gods." What Pilate said in mockery was utterly true. Jesus Christ is King. As Jesus underwent death before his exaltation, so must we. Our own path to glory, exaltation, and ultimate resurrection comes through a dying to self.

✦ What is the essential "truth" revealed by Jesus in the gospels?

Brief Silence

Prayer

Lord God, may these prayers we offer and our commitment to their fulfillment lead to the realization of your kingdom in our time and place, until the coming of our Redeemer and King, your Son, our Lord Jesus Christ, in whose name we offer these prayers. **Amen.**